Better Conversations for Better Results

A Leader's Guide to Skillful Work Conversations That are Purposeful, Powerful, and Pivotal

Lindiwe Stovall Lester

Author of *The Everyday Leader* and
The People Smart Leader

ISBN number: 978-1-7344826-8-3

Library of Congress Cataloguing-in-Publication Data

Lester, Lindiwe Stovall

Better Conversations for Better Results, A Leader's Guide to Skillful Work Conversations

- Leading People
- Business Management
- Personal Development
- Communication
- Workplace Culture
- People Skills

Cover design by Kozakura Publishing. For information or inquiries: info@pseinstitutebooks.com or www.pseinstitutebooks.com

I dedicate this book to my grandsons, Jide and Zaire, who I'm confident will one day be among our leaders. May you learn to use your voices for what's good and just on your journey to become fully realized little humans.

It's also dedicated to all those who agonized under leaders when we were still in the process of evolving, but not quite there.

table of

CONTENTS

If you are contemplating questions like the ones below, _Better Conversations for Better Results_ presents you with valuable options for responding and moving ahead.

Which of my conversations tend to go well?

Which ones leave others inspired?

Which ones leave people (and me) deflated?

How can I make them count for more?

Which type do I tend to avoid or get anxious about?

Why do I keep having the same conversations and they don't produce much?

How can I stop overtalking in my staff conversations?

What do the best conversationalists do?

How do I recognize and mitigate my conversation triggers?

What can I do about the impulse to be right and controlling?

How can I plan better conversations?

How do I manage myself better, so I bring my best to my interactions?

Better Conversations: The payoff

When we are skillful with our words, emotions, and thoughts in conversation, we are able to think creatively with others, build connections, deepen trust, inspire commitment, reduce stress, increase staff engagement, and exceed work expectations.

Bad conversations: The costs

When we have bad (i.e., *un*skillful) conversations, we can sap positive energy, decrease the potential to produce work excellence, set up a cycle of poor interactions, waste people's time and talents, and needlessly incur various costs.

Introduction

The Weight of the Leader's Conversations

"Use your words, honey," my daughter says to her five-year-old. When he couldn't easily figure out how to make the various puzzle pieces fit together, he became frustrated, sad, and began talking so rapidly she couldn't tell what he was saying.

"Slow down, you can figure this out; use your words and let's talk about this," mom says to him. As he slows his breathing and gets his words together, he relaxes, and his brain works to solve the puzzle. As he puts forth the new effort, mom asks him questions about what he needs and how he feels. He regains confidence and emotional control, then persists in solving the puzzle.

"Use your words" is now a mantra for this mom and child used when he gets overwhelmed and frustrated: Mom: *"What do you need to do?"* He responds: *"Calm down and use my words."*

How this book came to exist

Though the work of coaching leaders is more complex and nuanced than the opening mother and child story, I do see parallels. Leaders, in their attempts to exchange ideas, solve puzzles, address divergent thoughts, or get complex messages across with staff and colleagues, often need to be better using their words as they engage in these many consequential conversations.

This book extends from my previous two books (The Everyday Leader and The People Smart Leader) and from coaching engagements (i.e., conversations) over the last few years. Sessions with several clients turned to leaders' avoidance or poor execution of important, and potentially costly work conversations. One of the pivotal questions became: *What's the conversation you need to have, and what might that look like?*

Why another book about conversations?

Conversation is an aspect of communication. And **the higher you ascend, your conversations become more frequent, influential, and consequential.** That should be a signal for growth-oriented leaders to address what's referred to as their "conversational intelligence.[1]"

Effectively leading, participating in, or mediating conversations is often directly correlated to your and your team's overall performance, level of inspiration,

---

[1] Glaser, J. E. 2014. Conversational Intelligence: How Great Leaders Build Trust and Get Extraordinary Results.

efficiency, and work results. Skillful conversations can also build healthier relationships, develop people, help reach better decisions, and choose the best actions.

Conversations everywhere: You have conversations all day and year-round. Some are spontaneous, others planned, others that should have been planned, and still others that shouldn't have been held. Leaders converse with coworkers, direct reports, customers, partners, supervisors, colleagues, and more. We have text, email, phone, in-person, and video-conference conversations. Some of these are not that consequential while others can be pivotal for the organization, the career of staffers, the well-being of others, or the clarity of work. A pattern of poor conversations can establish a chaotic or unhealthy ethos that permeates the workplace.

There's good reason that much has been written about work conversations. We have conversation book titles that start with words such as: *Crucial, Fierce, Difficult, Powerful, Focused, Courageous, Critical, Worthwhile,* and more. What does that tell us? It is an indicator that this is a competency that has challenged leaders for a long time. I'm adding *Better* to the list, hoping to support leaders in a slightly different or reinforcing way.

What's distinctive about this book?

<u>Better Conversations for Better Results</u> offers content to expand your thinking about your conversations, so you don't take them for granted. The book also provides deliberate and practical ways to enhance your skills.

What I believe sets this book apart from the plethora of others is its brevity, real stories, and self-guided exercises that can dramatically elevate the quality of your conversations. The second half of the book offers simple, adaptable frameworks for the most vexing work conversations.

> *Since 50-80% of leader's time is spent in conversation, it's worth it to get better.*

According to various reports, leaders spend 50-80% of their time in conversation. So, I trust making these exchanges count for more is a worthy aim.

The "Better Conversation" effect

Most of the senior and mid-level leaders I come across in my coaching and consulting practice are, without question, talented. Nonetheless, they too often weaken the potency of their high-quality work through poor conversation practices and underdeveloped skills.

Take this example: One client, promoted to a C-suite role, a position she had worked hard to get, was upset that her pre-promotion work was not reassigned but appeared to be wrapped into the new role. She spent weeks steaming over this and finally said to me, *"I'm going to tell her she can't use me like that."* I replied: *"Whoa. Let's first acknowledge that you got the promotion you wanted. That's a win, right? Yes. Now, what's the issue? Let's define it. And, once we define it, let's talk through how a conversation about it may yield the best outcomes for you and your CEO."*

When she settled down and walked through the issues, they sounded to her like valid concerns to inquire about. I then asked, *"Why do you need this emotional build up to have the conversation? Could there be some things you haven't considered or know about that inquiring could answer for you?"* Over the next week, she calmly planned for and held the conversation. She later told me that it went well—that her manager was aware of the added burden and that she had already begun thinking about how to ease the workload.

The client's anxiety subsided, and she began to contemplate her underlying assumptions that may be keeping her from having more effective conversations. Some assumptions she agreed were holding her back:

   a.   *People are always and only out for themselves.*

   b.   *My view is typically reasonable, logical, singular, and right.*

   c.   *People won't understand my point of view.*

   d.   *The CEO might think I'm being unappreciative.*

This led to talking about a fundamental coaching idea— that people, including her, have often neglected using their internal resources to shift, reframe, even examine assumptions for better problem solving.

Strive for" better" not perfection

Many of us are driven, ambitious people who want to get things right all of the time. In conversation, however, it might be more useful to work on "better" and not perfection, lest we frustrate ourselves.

As humans, both logic and emotions are often at work, and the latter can complicate our interactions. People bring their accumulated experiences with them to work, and we are not always aware of what's at play or at stake emotionally with our conversation partners. Thus, we can say something, believed to be innocuous, that derails the interaction. In that moment, we had no way to predict the response.

As an example, *I recall one day as I sat and chatted casually with my brother, I made a sarcastic comment, that immediately shifted his smile to a tightened face and a diatribe about how I make comments that he saw as offensive. I had no idea. I felt bad; but the exchange taught me about the triggering effect of certain comments I make. Further, I learned more about what mattered to him. In the moment, I attempted to explain my intentions and tried not to be defensive. It was hard, but I took a breath. It turned out "better," not perfect.*

That's why striving for better might beat perfection. We are human, with emotional fluidity, so how we each engage and react are not fully predictable.

Own your power to change your conversations

For leaders, conversation effectiveness requires believing that you have both power and responsibility for how you lead and the outcomes that result from it. It follows then that when conversations go wrong and begin to devolve, we take responsibility; we don't externalize and blame others (using words like *they, them,* or *it*—did or caused it*).*

This ownership attitude empowers us to do something about our words and actions. It doesn't deny that it may be helpful to understand the patterns, politics, and policies that influence your work context. This is recognition that dwelling on those does not prompt you to have the right conversations to own and solve problems or mitigate the obstructions.

Honing your skills related to how you engage in dialogue at work is within your control and will benefit you and others. Better conversation skills empower you to take charge of yourself in ways you may not have given much consideration to. This development asks you to act and observe yourself in pursuit of better results, personal satisfaction, increased skills, and overall enhanced leadership demeanor.

In the spheres of control, as described by Stephen Covey[2], people inclined to be proactive flourish more by looking inward (where we have more control) than on looking outward at external factors where we have limited or no control.

CONTROL✓

thoughts, mood, reactions, decisions, words, time, actions, etc.

---

[2] Covey, S. 1989. Seven Habits of Highly Effective People.

By focusing effort on what Covey sees as the **sphere of control,** we purposefully allocate our time and work on such areas as our thought patterns, beliefs, actions, moods, words, reactions, decisions, and use of our time. These are key areas for building conversational intelligence. Own your power to change things by changing your conversation behaviors and mindset.

What's inside?

This book is a personal guide to help you know and grow yourself through deliberate conversation competency development. You will learn the extent to which your conversation quality either moves you, others, and the organization forward or impedes positive momentum. There are stories, reflection pages, practice and sample conversations, self-assessments, questions for better inquiry, tips for deeper listening, and strategies for higher quality advocacy for your ideas.

There are five chapters:

The first chapter makes the case for WHY to become more conversationally adept, the necessary skills and behaviors, and the types of conversations worth having due to their potential to advance or hinder progress.

Chapters 2 and 3 become more personal; they are designed for you to honor your current competencies and increase conversational self-awareness. They allow you to pull back the curtain to reflect on and diagnose what drives your conversation practices and habits, where you are already strong, and help you identify improved approaches specific to your needs.

Chapters 4 and 5 assume half of the book's pages. They offer better and powerful conversation elements, processes, and examples. Chapter 5 includes ten (10) adaptable conversation templates, and worksheets to plan your own conversations.

Get started.

I suggest you read the first section to establish a positive, productive mindset for entering into high-yield, high quality conversations. Or, if you have an upcoming high-stakes conversation or a type that usually triggers you, go directly to Chapters 4 and 5 to work on your mindset and that specific conversation. On the next page, you can jumpstart your better conversation practice by pre-thinking six questions.

By the way, in the two years it has taken me to finish this little book, my grandson, now seven, is still reminded during his moments of frustration to "Use your words." What we discover is that can mean using them more, better, less, clearer, louder, quieter, or kinder.

One habit that can change your conversations now

Before every IMPORTANT conversation, take at least a few minutes to answer these six questions:

---

1. **WHY** am I having this conversation?

2. **WHAT** are the best outcomes I want from this conversation (for me AND my conversation partner)?

3. What **INFORMATION** am I using that makes this conversation important? Is it factual, hearsay, an assumption, a feeling?

4. **HOW** should I structure it to make the best use of the time allotted?

5. At the end of the meeting, what **RESULTS** or next steps do I want to leave with?

6. **SELF-MANAGEMENT**: How will I situate myself – my emotions, body, and voice- to bring my best to the conversation?

Chapter 4 provides more details to help you reflect on each of these questions.

Chapter 1

Conversations are often THE work

This chapter encourages leaders to prioritize increasing their conversation aptitude, since power, influence, and meaning are embedded in the abundance of leaders' exchanges at work.

If it's true that between 50 and 80% of a leader's time at work is consumed in conversations, and considering leaders' salaries, that's some pretty expensive talking. That's reason enough to ask: *If I'm spending this much time, how effective are my conversations, and how can I optimize them to achieve more for me and the team?*

> *"The most important work in the new economy is creating conversations.[3]"*

---

[3] Weber, A. What's So New About the New Economy? HBR Feb. 1993

The power of the leader's voice

Consider all of the things you say as you go about your day, much of which you may forget right after you utter the words. Yet, others, especially those you supervise, may catalogue those seemingly harmless words.

There are plenty stories of people becoming fixated on just one of a person's remarks among many, such as *"I don't think you're ready for that." "I didn't think what you said was profound at all." "You don't seem capable of that level of thinking." "I'm not impressed with your report." "You are my lowest performing employee." "What's wrong with you? Everybody else gets it."*

For you, these blunt or careless remarks may hold little lasting value. Yet they can stick with others. Leaders' words are infused with power to affect others (and outcomes). They can cause people to form perceptions about you, your style, your capabilities, and your values. Your words can also affect others' self-perceptions, self-confidence, self-worth, and overall well-being.

> *"There is little connection between the time it takes to say the words and the lasting impact they may have on a person, a relationship, or an organization."*[4]

This understanding alone should signal a need to prioritize building skills for masterful conversations.

---

[4] Glaser, J. E., 2014. Conversational Intelligence: How Great Leaders Build Trust and Get Extraordinary Results. P. xiii

What work do you want your conversation to do?

Since conversations are a major part of a leader's work, there's value in considering the specific work we want our conversations to achieve.

Since conversations are work and resource consuming, we ought to consider the specific work we want our conversations to do.

I partnered with a leader who couldn't grasp why she might need to rethink her words to make them more palatable to her supervising manager. She believed changing her tone and words would compromise her authentic voice. We then examined what she meant by authentic—is it saying whatever she wanted, how she wanted, to be completely unfiltered without restraint? As she reflected on this, she conceded "That's kind of silly, isn't it?"

A recent publication explores the problem with a leader bringing their whole, raw, or authentic, self to work. It calls for maintaining professional boundaries rather than establishing a pattern of unfiltered interactions:

> *"Authenticity is the modern leader's favorite cologne: applied heavily, performed loudly and often confused with actual depth...Being authentic isn't the same as being effective. In fact, psychological science suggests that most effective leaders are anything but unfiltered."*[5]

---

[5] Chamorro-Premuzic, T., Why leaders should bring their best self, not their whole self, to work. HBR, July 31, 2025.

Another author speaks about authenticity in this way:

> *"Authenticity is definitely not just mindlessly reacting in whatever way feels good in the moment. To be an authentic communicator, we have to know what we believe and then we have to act in a way that is consistent with those beliefs. The journey toward having better conversations, therefore, is actually a journey toward authenticity."*[6]

An awakening came once I asked her: *What do you want this conversation to do?* She responded: *I want the conversation to help us find ways to interact honestly, directly, and with each of us feeling heard and respected when our viewpoints differ.* We explored that we are each expansive human beings with many communication options that allow us to remain our authentic selves.

When we calmly probe what we want to achieve through our conversations, we can bring our authentic voice into the dialogue—constructively and humanely. That's what happened for her and with productive effects.

What is a conversation? What's not?

A conversation is a type or aspect of communication. It is often distinct from, while similar to, other forms of communication (such as written, visual, nonverbal).

Here are two definitions of <u>conversation</u>:

---

[6] Knight, J. 2016. Better Conversations: Coaching Ourselves and Each Other to Be More Credible, Caring, and Connected, p. 7.

"Conversations are dynamic, interactive, and inclusive. They evolve and impact the way we connect, engage, interact, and influence others, enabling us to shape reality, mind-sets, events, and outcomes in a collaborative way."[7]

"A conversation occurs when people talk to each other... You listen closely and respond appropriately, so that your conversation is a true exchange of ideas, not just people waiting for their turn to talk. A good conversation makes you feel heard, satisfied, and maybe even more informed."[8]

Most common features: You will know you are in a conversation if the following are evident: (The **quality** of the conversation can be further enriched when other attributes and skills are also operating—See Chapters 2 and 3):

- There's a verbal exchange between two or more people. Thoughts, feelings, and observations are expressed, questioned are asked and answered, and/or information is shared back and forth.

- It's interactive- i.e., there is turn taking.

- Involves a shift from monologue to dialogue—i.e., from talking *to* or *at* to talking *with*.

- There's improvising, meaning ideas and thoughts are generated in the moment, which can't be addressed by behaving in a scripted manner.

---

[7] Glaser, J. pg. xiii
[8] Vocabulary.com

Peter Senge, systems scientist and author of <u>Fifth Discipline</u>[9], further distinguishes dialogue from simply talking or discussion. In discussion, he says people with opposing views are setting out to win rather than learn. In dialogue exchanges, people set out to understand, to enlarge ideas, and gain insight to find better solutions for shared issues.

> *We are not in a conversation when in the modes of telling, presenting, one-way endless talking, commanding.*

What's not a conversation? The above descriptions help us distinguish real conversations from incomplete or quasi-ones. Anytime we are in the mode of one-way talking, presenting, persuading, stating one's case, even commanding and telling, we are *not* in a conversation. (Without a doubt, there are times when making direct, non-negotiable statements is the best approach; this book is only related to times when our intent is to have *actual* conversations.)

On occasion, leaders have shared how they addressed a concern with a staffer, saying, *"I talked to them about it."* Yet, when I probed about the staffer's response and receptivity (i.e., "How did they respond?"), they couldn't say. There was no action, decision, or agreement. These are incomplete conversations with two people talking without settling the issue being addressed.

---

[9] Senge, P. M. The Fifth Discipline, The Art and Practice of the Learning Organization. 2006 edition.

Without clear closure, people easily leave with varying versions of what was said and confusion about the next steps. They may depart with thoughts like, "What just happened?" or "I still don't know what's next."

An incomplete conversation example:

Principal: *Once again, I spent an hour telling the teachers they need to be present for their hall duties during class breaks, and they still don't show up.*

Me: *Why did it take an hour to deliver that message? And what was their response to it?*

Principal: *I didn't ask for a response; I spent a lot of time giving examples, trying to talk sternly, and explaining.*

Me: *Let's walk through the structure of a conversation that might help you get closer to the results you want. Think about how to be clear, efficient, and determine what they need to get it done. Can you pause, relax, ask for their thoughts and input, then give them time to respond, confirm their understanding and the next steps?*

Principal: *That doesn't sound like an hour meeting, but less than 30 minutes for a conversation with clear actions. It didn't cross my mind that I never made space for them to offer their thoughts and confirm what they would do differently to address the issue at hand.*

The next time she raised the same topic, she spent 20 minutes on it, gathered their thoughts, and ended with agreements and verbal commitments to change the behavior. She learned that they preferred a schedule of assignments to this duty rather than asking everybody to do this task every day. That seemed to work better.

I also think of *quasi-conversations* as those we think are conversations but only amount to quasi, i.e., *sort of*. They may have all the basic components yet miss elements that make them meaningful. For example, they may lack a clear purpose, be unfocused, or have a menacing tone.

Shifting from quasi or incomplete conversations to genuine two-way dialogue focused on something worthwhile requires thinking about: *Am I going to have a conversation or just state my case?*

Here's an example of a leader making the shift:

"I realize I was initially always telling my people what to do, assuming I was an expert, and they were not. This created problems in that my staff told me they didn't feel heard or respected. I began to do more listening and acknowledging their points of view. That made a difference. Now one staffer who I said was undermining me, I am now helping them get moved to a VP level."

Another instance of non-conversation is the use of rhetorical questions or overused expressions that sound like questions. Infusing "You know what I mean?" throughout a monologue is not dialogue, especially since little space is opened for the other person to answer. It's a habit that grows out of a lack of confidence, anxiety about what you are saying, or need for affirmation.

Most common types of work conversations

Management publications and my experiences indicate the following as recurring themes of leaders' work conversations. Most are related to their direct reports.

1. Setting and clarifying priorities
2. Performance planning and appraisal (quick check ins, quarterly, annual, recalibrating it)
3. Building relationships (e.g., understanding strengths, motivators, and preferences; building cross function collaboration; repairing breaches)
4. Performance improvement issues
5. Decisions (sharing and responses to them)
6. Recognition/honoring valued contributions
7. Addressing changes or sharing tough decisions
8. Delegating assignments
9. Coaching feedback about blind spots, poor behavior
10. Incidents
11. Team and other kinds of meetings
12. Dissenting points of view
13. Inspiration during tough times
14. To unite the staff around a goal or issue
15. Salary negotiation
16. Mediating staff conflicts
17. Turning rivals into allies
18. Input on how leader can get better
19. Project status/updates, progress check ins
20. Inappropriate or unprofessional conduct
21. Corrective feedback, work mistakes
22. Career development, retention conversations

Of those above, which are your most frequent types of challenging interactions? Circle the numbers.

List any other types of conversation you tend to have:

_____

_____

(You can adapt the conversation templates in Chapter 5 to be *better* with all of these types.)

The cost of bad or avoided conversations

There are untold costs associated with leaders who are low-skill conversationalists. Review the following list to think about the varying ways that inattention to your interactions may be costing you and your team.

- ☒ Confusion
- ☒ Misinterpretation
- ☒ Hard feelings
- ☒ Frustration
- ☒ Overwork or wrong work
- ☒ Assumptions spread
- ☒ Staffers feel unappreciated
- ☒ Repetition of the same topics
- ☒ No resolutions
- ☒ Diminished performance
- ☒ Erosion of trust
- ☒ No learning
- ☒ Unhealthy culture emerges
- ☒ Issues get beyond fixing
- ☒ Staff departures
- ☒ Gossip becomes an accepted norm

What conversation do YOU need to have that you're avoiding? Plan it. Have it. Avoid the excessive cost of putting it off.

Look at this example of the myriad costs of this overly-kind, conflict avoidant leader's failure to have a needed candid conversation.

Lacking the courage to have a long-avoided tough conversation, the CEO's situation eventually became untenable. Ultimately the results were disappointing and highly emotional for him, a specific vice president on his team, and the team.

What tipped the scale was when the CEO did not promote the VP after a year-long restructuring led to elevated roles for several of the VP's peers. The VP became upset and even used profanity with the CEO, about not getting a similar promotion. Instead of remaining true to the plan, the CEO, not having an appropriate thoughtful response, assured the VP he would consider it in 6-9 months (despite his belief she hadn't performed in a way to warrant it.)

This was a wrong conversation that would have implications later. Over the next several months, the VP expected his support to be ready for the higher role and didn't feel she was getting it. She pouted, berated him, and gossiped with colleagues. Finally, he admitted to me (and her) that he had no plan of offering the role to her (with valid reasons), but he was fearful of having to deal with her hostile reaction. Then nine months of ineffective, often volatile engagements, public disrespect, and his evasive interactions ended with this VP's emotionally charged exit from the organization.

Some of the costs for him and the organization: *confusion, hard feelings, unhealthy cultural norms, issues beyond repair, diminished trust, spread of assumptions, and loss of employment.*

I did an exercise with him on deconstructing and reconstructing that first conversation (See the exercise in Chapter 4). This helped him prepare for the separation conversation. It was also a lesson in the value of better, timely, honest conversations.

> *"The very outcomes we fear if we confront someone's behavior are practically guaranteed to show up if we don't. It will just take longer..."*[10]

Benefits: A place beyond wasted words and time

Effectively engaging in key conversations offers advantages for your organization, enhances your credibility and more. Quality dialogues can:

- Increase employee motivation
- Support healthier team dynamics
- Help bring clarity about direction you're going
- Reduce redundant conversations
- Improve work outcomes
- Uncover people's motivators, values, style preference, and unique talents
- Enhance relationships and trust
- Be a means for staff engagement
- Foster staff growth and sharpen skills
- Give you access to information, feelings, and perspectives to inform how you lead others

[10] Scott. S. 2004. Fierce Conversations. P. 137

- Reduce stress, for you and the other person
- Help overcome biases in people's thinking
- Clarify whether your assumptions are based in reality or not
- Contribute to a healthier work culture
- Lead to more informed decision-making

Closing Reflection: Think about three of your recent conversations, and rate how productive you feel they were: (1-lowest, 10-excellent)

Conversation with	About	Rating
1.		
2.		
3.		

What worked for you? _____

_____

What would you like to improve? _____

_____

The big question Chapter 1 posed for your internal response related to your weighty conversations: What *work* do I want this conversation to do? Then plan and execute it in ways that *allow the conversation to do that work.*

Chapter 2

What Effective Conversationalists Know and Do

This chapter looks at what leaders who exhibit conversational effectiveness know and do. You will also be nudged to do the work to have increasingly *better* interactions for better and meaningful results.

Conversational effectiveness is a differentiating competency that separates an average leader from a highly skilled one. Despite your time pressures to set vision, operationalize plans, put out fires, develop staff, and manage complexity, upgrading your conversations will elevate your leadership stature.

> *"We believe a major reason change efforts so often fail is that successful implementation eventually requires people to have difficult conversations—and they are not prepared to manage them skillfully."*[11]

---

[11] Stone, D, Patton, B, Heen, S. 2010. Difficult Conversations, p. xii

Exceptional conversationalists' qualities

Leaders with highly attuned conversation skills have been deliberate about developing and showing up at work with these qualities:

1. *Strong Emotional Intelligence*	Good self-awareness and emotional self-regulation along with attunement with others and skillful people management
2. *Candid and humane*	Deliver messages truthfully, clearly, and directly while balancing them with empathy
3. *Curious*	Seek learning, show interest, ask insightful questions rather than trying to prove their "smarts"
4. *Behaviorally flexible*	Situationally modulate tone and energy; capable of and willing to change their mind in light of new information
5. *Good at setting context*	Take a big picture perspective on conversation issues, connecting issues to the needs of the individual and organization; neither petty nor trivial
6. *Address individual motivators*	Recognize differences in the ways people are motivated and integrate that into how they engage in conversation
7. *Show restraint and patience*	Slow down, as needed, to involve others and to broaden their thinking; avoid impulsivity
8. *Take responsibility*	Tend not to blame external factors for issues; can admit mistakes and move forward
9. *Low defensiveness*	Do not get drawn into endless back and forth to prove their rightness; they listen, seek solutions, and move forward.

10. Conflict skills	Demonstrate an intelligent approach to engaging in, valuing, and resolving conflict
11. Deep listening	Seek understanding and can embrace silence, allowing time to think and process
12. Present	Are undistracted by outside activity while in conversations
13. Discernment	Have a keen sense of what's too much or too little, right timing, appropriate language, etc.
14. Ethos of human equality	Don't flaunt their status, show maturity, reveal their story and setbacks as appropriate
15. Focus	Keep attention on the topic at hand, redirecting as needed when things veer off track
16. Respect and invite other views	Assess their own perspective and thinking by seeking and hearing opposing or new perspectives
17. Decisive	Don't shift their stance based on every whim; they support their case and stand strong as needed.
18. Understand drivers of performance	Aware of what people need to do their best work (e.g., feedback, tools, incentives, etc.); look for and work to remove barriers
19. Good mental model for conversations	Are instinctively competent in how to engage in conversation, use a proven framework
20. Accountability drive	Don't lose sight of achieving work results even as they balance inclusion and empathy

Of the 20 items, which do you believe are your areas of demonstrated top strengths? Highlight them.

When you get to Chapter 3, you will revisit much of what's in this chart to more precisely identify your areas of current competence and areas to enhance.

More on three of exceptional conversationalist qualities: The next paragraphs amplify three qualities from the table above: strong EQ, conflict skills, and conversation mental model.

Strong EQ: Emotional Management and Agility

You probably already know that IQ refers to your intellectual capacity (or quotient), which measures problem solving, logic, and analytical thinking. EQ, another intelligence, is about emotional competence. It addresses emotional self-awareness and self-regulation along with social skills, social dynamics, and empathy (i.e., how you engage others). Most leaders have likely invested in developing their IQ through education and experience—decisive factors in hiring and promotions. Yet underdeveloped EQ is a key culprit in leadership derailment once on the job.

A leader with high-level self-awareness and good habits of emotional self-regulation is less prone to have conversations that go awry or nowhere at all. They can sense other's emotional currents, imagine what they might be experiencing, and choose how to manage themselves accordingly. *In the moment*, they demonstrate what Susan David, psychologist and author of Emotional Agility (2016), describes here:

"Being emotionally agile involves being sensitive to context and responding to the world as it is right now."

They don't deny their emotions; they purposely flex their internal sensations. They shift their tone, thought process, energy, and more to match the situation to help ensure more effective interactions. They also recognize and adjust well to social cues and diverse cultural frameworks (i.e., they "read the room"), and they inspire others in various settings.

Dr. Alec Mercer, human behavioralist, of the fictional television show, The Irrational, highlighted how emotional intelligence plays into conversation quality. He told his team: *"Think about the emotions you are trying to bring out in others because that's what drives behavior.[12]"* In essence, when in conversation, if you want the person to feel hopeful, supported, and not debilitated or distressed, consider whether your words and tone help evoke the emotions that drive towards the outcomes you seek.

High EQ leaders are known to shift tone, thought process, and energy to match the situation and ensure better engagement.

Emotional self-regulation never means an absence of emotion since emotions are hallmarks of humanity. They are always at work, whether joy, contentment, disappointment, sadness, anger, or delight. Your aim

---

[12] NBC. Season 2, Episode 16, March 2025.

is to figure out when your emotions are supporting your and others' best interests and, if not, take a moment to modulate or regroup if triggered.

Watch yourself for these "low EQ" indicators: If you see or feel yourself showing any of these while in conversation, it's a signal to adjust "in the moment":

- Emotional outbursts or runaway emotions
- Turning attention to yourself..." I, I, I..."
- Taking credit for other's successes
- Low empathy
- Blaming others and finger pointing
- Over-talking, leaving the other person out for lengthy periods
- Obliviousness to others' feelings
- Difficulty "reading the room," i.e., picking up social cues
- Pushing too hard to be *right*

Skills for conflict in conversations

The leader who is adept at facilitating conversations that move conflict situations to their best resolution typically has strong emotional intelligence (along with other skills). They don't fear conflict since they know it is inevitable. They also recognize the benefits (e.g., learning and better solutions) which can derive from it when approached in a healthy way.

Conflict is described as competing, unreconciled or clashing views, interests, or expectations between people often accompanied by strong emotions.

To effectively reconcile conflict conversations, leaders need to possess Conflict Intelligence (C.I.), says Professor Peter Coleman.[13] He pinpoints four skills a leader needs to manage and resolve workplace conflict (similar to those I presented in The People Smart Leader Chapter 5):

1. *Self-awareness and self-regulation*, to recognize and manage your reactions so you remain calm, steady, and focused.

2. *Strong social-conflict skills*; those include deep listening, balancing advocating one's position with collaboration, and checking biases to help move towards constructive, mutually accepted solutions.

> *Social-conflict skills, big picture wisdom and situational adaptability are needed to manage conflict-ridden conversations.*

3. *Situational adaptivity*, that is knowing how to tailor your strategies to fit several types of conflicts and discerning when to lean in or step back and adjust for cultural considerations.

4. *Systemic wisdom*, to see the big picture, embrace complexity, and consider learning from the past to address deeply rooted conflicts.

Unresolved conflicts have an excessive cost, so skillfulness in managing these conversations will be worth it. Coleman notes costs such as excessive executive turnover and that "...*contentious interactions*

---

[13] Coleman, P. T., The Conflict-Intelligent Leader, HBR, July/August 2025

at work are estimated to cost businesses more than $2billion a day in productivity losses and absenteeism."

Astute leaders preemptively and continuously develop a team culture that includes conflict and collaboration skill building and healthy workplace behavioral norms. This enables conflict intelligence among those in the conflict, which decreases the need for your intervention.

Conversation mental models

The use of helpful mental models when in dialogue seems to be deficient in many interactions. Here's one lived experience of no or poor mental models for how a fairly successful meeting conversation happens:

Nearly every month, I observe a board meeting that meanders into minutiae, pet peeves, arguments, violations of behavior protocols, and more. All of this happens without anyone redirecting the session back to the agenda with its suggested timeframes. Without exception, I rarely make it through the entire meeting. By the time I left a recent one, the meeting had already gone on for three hours, people were frustrated, audibly whispering and sighing, and leaving one by one. What was the leader thinking? Apparently, he had no mental model for how an effective board meeting works.

Important conversations should have a constructive mental model at its foundation to help ensure better results. **Mental models are frameworks, mental**

pictures, even acronyms, we call upon to view, understand, make decisions, take action, and process things. We acquire them through experience, education, cultural standards, and other influences. We all have them and use them in different situations.

There are myriad models on conversation stages to help people move through them with intention and focus. Below are some of the well-known mental models people rely upon during conversations:

- *Active Listening:* a process to help us be present using such behaviors as eye contact, listening, and paraphrasing

- *The Ladder of Inference:* to help separate assumptions from facts, and seek clarity to avoid drawing erroneous conclusions

- *SCARF:* people internalize this model's acronym—Status, Certainty, Autonomy, Relatedness and Fairness—to remind them to address these factors that motivate human behavior when communicating.

In my personal mental model for meetings, I look for a statement of purpose for a gathering, expressions of what the conveners hope to achieve by the end, items on the agenda that relate to that purpose, closure that lets us know whether we achieved our purpose and decisions on next steps in pursuit of it.

Caveat-Don't get stuck! Mental models sometimes need to change or call us to adjust, especially if they are not leading us where we need to go. I admit I am, at times, challenged when my expectations are not addressed. So, I have to practice a bit of behavioral flexibility. The point is: Have one in mind when in conversation, while recognizing there may be times when they can cause over-reliance on our way, biases against other approaches, and resistance to change.

Here's a simplified conversation model I propose and develop further in Chapters 4 and 5.

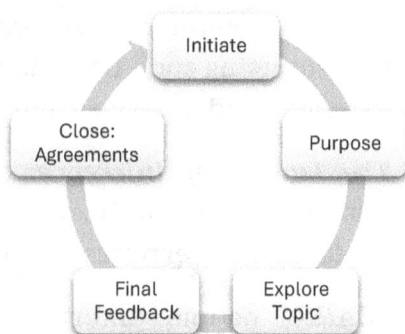

Initiate

Purpose

Close: Agreements

Explore Topic

Final Feedback

Some signs of leader conversation discomfort and skill deficiency

- ☒ Constant talking, with few pauses
- ☒ Lack of curiosity or interest in other viewpoints
- ☒ Lack of focus
- ☒ Dismissiveness
- ☒ Using wrong tone
- ☒ Inconsiderate of cultural factors

- ☒ Soften or obscure the message
- ☒ Wrong type
- ☒ Indirect and ambiguous messages
- ☒ Putting it off too long
- ☒ Lack of candor
- ☒ Losing sight of the point

- ☒ Overall avoidance of conversation
- ☒ Useless, repetitive phrases... "you know what I mean?"
- ☒ Not seeking others' views
- ☒ Changing voice quality
- ☒ Overconfidence in one's viewpoint
- ☒ Focus on winning, not resolution
- ☒ Exaggerating..." you always..." "you never"
- ☒ Relying heavily on positional authority
- ☒ Inflexible in your perspective
- ☒ Monologue
- ☒ No eye contact
- ☒ Rambling on and on
- ☒ Lacking the needed facts

Reflection: Take a moment to **circle** those you tend to display when uncomfortable in conversation. Any others for you? _____

Conversations that go wrong and which are worth having

The above signs of discomfort also point to the reasons some conversations go wrong. Sometimes conversations are not useful, valuable, or they derail due to bad timing, wrong tone, no closure or even inadvertently having the wrong type. So, if the conversation is about, e.g., gathering input, be clear that it's not for decision-making. If the conversation is about evaluating work, don't spend all the time on career development. **Keep the main thing the main thing for the good of all parties.**

One example of a conversation gone wrong was due to one senior leader's discomfort addressing behavioral concerns. This resulted in the leader having the wrong type of conversation.

The leader had shared with me that he was having conversations with a key staffer about a pattern of behavior that adversely affected the leadership team's dynamics. He was thoughtful, organized his message, engaged in dialogue with the staffer, and assumed the staffer would take the appropriate steps. That didn't happen; she missed the signal that these changes were critical and could lead to departure if not addressed.

*As the leader and I talked later, it became clear that the staffer saw the conversation as a **support conversation** rather than a **performance conversation**. He had interjected far too many accolades about her talents and contributions such that the critical behavioral change items came across to her as "nice to dos" rather than "urgent" and "decisive" must dos.*

> *A leader's conversation discomfort leads to conversations going wrong, repetitiveness, little results, and high costs.... all reasons to get better.*

Eventually, the leader began to recognize that he had not only engaged in the wrong kind of conversation, but he also sent unintended messages which he then had to undo. He revisited the conversation after some months, being clearer and direct. Thereafter, she began shifting her behaviors in ways that allowed her contributions to yield more of what was expected of her.

The lesson: When the situation is urgent, critical, and possibly job-impacting, it is rarely useful to mix positive and critical feedback in the same conversation. This can send mixed signals, dilute the message, and come across as insincere.

Again, be mindful that repeated conversations that yield little results are in fact, conversations that have gone wrong, and they can be costly.

Discerning conversations worth having. When should you invest in them? **Not everything requires a conversation.** There are times when directly sharing information or giving a directive is sufficient. On the other hand, there are many conversations that need to occur, and others that shouldn't occur. So, think about which conversations are worth having.

It might be helpful to explore these questions internally before having any potentially high-risk conversation: *What's at stake? What if I don't have the conversation? Anything lost? Anything gained? How will it contribute to our work? Is this better left unsaid? Are there any biases at work that draw me to this conversation (e.g., style, personality, or generation)?*

The latter question about biases reminds me of something a dear friend says often to remind her to open herself to different perspectives. *"My story is not the only version."*

Too often, we assume everyone thinks (or should) the same as we do. Yet each of us brings the whole of our experiences with us into every conversation—our beliefs, values, worldviews, hurts and pains, joys, and triumphs. These influence how we engage with others, and being aware of that helps us pay attention to our thinking and adapt as needed.

"We all have biases, errors in judgment, and gaps in our thinking. But we're not very good at identifying them, and we're even worse at dealing with them."[14]

Conversations worth having meet most of these:

- Have a bearing on getting the work done or on the health of the team
- Are geared towards generating information, learning, or possible paths forward
- Have topics that require *mutual* engagement
- Address issues that can be resolved or yield what's expected (outcome-oriented)
- Include the right people to address the issues
- Involve data, thoughts, and feelings to reach a new place of understanding or agreement
- Take place at the right time

Look at this request a leader made:

Leader: Can you make space to coach my COO? He is pretty rough with people, and I've been getting complaints over the last year or so.

---

[14] Dubin, M. 2025. Blindspotting: How to See What's Holding You Back as a Leader, p.2

Me: Does your COO know about the complaints or the areas you'd like to see improved?

Leader: I think so...

Me: What does that mean? Have you talked WITH him about it and shared why it matters?

Leader: Not directly... I've been concerned he might feel offended if I bring it up.

Me: Would he be surprised if you raised the subject of the complaints?

Leader: Probably...

Me: Before deciding coaching is the solution, let's see if we can plan a well-executed conversation between the two of you. That conversation and follow-up support from you may eliminate any need for outside services.

So, we worked on the leader preparing his mind and the structure for a conversation that would both clarify and support the needed changes for this valued staffer. That conversation resulted in commitment to work on specific behaviors meant to demonstrate respect and mature approaches for collaborating with peers. Several months later, the leader confirmed things were coming along well. No money was spent on coaching; the aims were accomplished through several quality conversations.

This leader's conversation avoidance might indicate he was afflicted with what author of <u>Radical Candor</u> calls *ruinous empathy*. That is:

"to be so fixated on a person's feeling in the moment that you don't tell them something they'd be better knowing in the long run."[15]

Empathy is powerful but this type of "empathetic" avoidance can hurt far more than it helps.

Planning doesn't make perfect; it makes better

Well-planned conversations are those that clarify intentions, help you stay focused, consider how to keep you present, receptive, and thoughtful, and avoid your common landmines.

That being said, just because you plan doesn't mean the conversation will turn out exactly as you desired. The reason is our humanness, our experiences, our values, and our emotions are always operating in the background. **These make formulas imperfect and imprecise when in conversations. The human element can throw a monkey wrench into the best laid plans,** but planning is more likely to yield better conversations.

So, as you plan, remember to orient your mindset, tone, and energy; know what type of conversation you are having; check your biases; apply a mental model; and demonstrate regard for your partner in the conversation. Chapter 4 is a useful resource for planning better conversations.

---

[15] Scott, K. p. xii. 2019

Chapter 3

It's Personal: Assessing and Enhancing Your Conversations

This third chapter is all about the quality and effects of YOUR conversations. It guides you to clarify your *current* patterns and habits, along with target areas as you move to a *future* of better conversations.

Chapter 1 noted that leaders' conversations are more durable than they might think. Your words can stick with your staff and others for a long time, influencing them positively or adversely.

There are countless testimonies about the positive, supportive influence of a conversation on a person's life and view of their career trajectory. *"When Valerie said I had so much potential to be a team lead, I began to think differently about my goals. She inspired me."*

Leaders, whether teacher, manager, parent, or others occupying a "superior" role, also have interactions causing long lasting, debilitating effects on the conversation partner (e.g., deflated self-esteem or confidence, withdrawal, decreased performance, or worsening health). What makes these remarks most harmful is when they're offered without a sound rationale, human empathy, or ideas for development.

In light of the potency and durability of a leader's words, this next section offers an opportunity to reflect on and examine whether your conversations inspire and propel forward or deflate and diminish.

My current conversation process

With the frenetic pace of many workplaces, leaders can conduct their routine tasks performatively. Knowing that conversations are part of a leader's real work, it might be useful to stop and reflect on them.

Respond to the items below to get a sense of your "current" state of conversation.

1) What are my most common types of work conversations? _____
   _____
   _____
   _____

2) Which are the easiest for me to have? _____
   _____
   _____

3) Which are the most difficult? _____

_____

_____

4) Do I have a general practice I use to engage in important conversations? Y__ N__

5) If so, describe it here. _____

_____

_____

6) What are my voice and tone typically like when I engage in uncomfortable conversations? _____

_____

_____

You can examine other aspects of your interactions using the next few pages.

Patterns, tone, tenor, and assumptions

Patterns: I've been told my helpful patterns during conversations include showing real interest, asking useful questions, using both supporting and challenging language, and conveying empathy and encouragement. My unhelpful patterns, for example, are explaining more than necessary, sometimes wavering when I should stay on point, using sarcasm rather than being clear, and getting tired of listening to the point of not listening fully. My husband can offer more thoughts on my unconstructive habits.

Make a few notes about your patterns. If you're courageous, have someone who knows you well also offer input.

> **Think about this:** What message(s) are you conveying through your words and tone during conversations?

Tone and tenor: People are living, feeling beings. As such, the tone, mood, and emotions that underpin your messages will have an impact on the quality of your conversations.

What message(s) are you sending through your words and tone? Which (or other) of the statements below describe what your tone conveys in most conversations? (Depending on the subject and heft of the conversation, your tone will likely differ, while still remaining humane and respectful.)

- ○ "I support you and want you to succeed."
- ○ "I understand what you are facing, and I am here to help get to a solution."
- ○ "The work matters much more than you and your feelings or issues."
- ○ "I value your thoughts, and I'm listening."
- ○ "My time is valuable, so let's get to it."
- ○ "I think you're bad at your job, and I want to be sure you know it."

○ "I'm your boss, you're my subordinate."
○ "What you think doesn't matter, just listen to me."

One of my clients, in a moment of clarity, remarked: *"I always have judgment in my tone. I need to explore why I feel the need to do that, then fix it and be able to get my message across better."*

The point here is, according to Glaser,

> *"Conversations carry meaning—and meaning is embedded in the listener even more than in the speaker."*[16]

Assumptions embedded in your conversations: A set of assumptions and beliefs is always operating in the background of our lives and interactions. They are unavoidable, and they are the lenses through which we interpret people's actions and more. Some of these serve us well, while others impede learning and resolution. What assumptions do you typically bring to your conversations? How have these been useful? How might these bias your receptivity to other perspectives, especially those brought by direct reports or colleagues?

Everyone makes general assumptions about life and people, and there are those related to the specific situations about which you are having conversations. In an exchange with a friend, he was emphatic that, *"Most people are manipulative and out for themselves, not to be trusted."* Though he said he maintains

---

[16] Glaser, J. E. 2014. Conversational Intelligence: How Great Leaders Build Trust and Get Extraordinary Results. P. xiii

relationships with people, he sees them through that stance on human nature. I offered this, *"I believe most people are well-intended, though self-interest can take precedence when they can't find a win-win approach."* That didn't work him.

Here are other examples of general and workplace-related assumptions I've heard:

- People hate feedback.
- People want to do well at work.
- People are always trying to get away with something.
- Older employees will never change.
- Younger employees are slackers.
- Work is not meant to be fun.
- Work should be fun.
- If I don't watch them, they won't do their work.
- With effort, most problems can be solved.
- This is going to be a messy interaction.
- He doesn't agree because he wants my job.
- She is undermining me because she's jealous of me.

So, assumptions and beliefs affect our conversations. Knowing ours 1) helps us recognize when our biases are disadvantaging us and others, and 2) can signal a need to dial back on our impulsive perspectives on issues. In essence, we need to expand how we view ourselves and others. Susan Scott uses these words:

> *"If we are to develop as leaders...our very identities must become fluid."*[17]

---

[17] Scott, S. Fierce Conversations. p. 75

Sharpening your skills

Now, look at your current interaction strengths and skills and those you need for better conversations.

Assess skillset and mindset for effective conversations. This list is closely akin to the list in Chapter 2.

Indicate the ones where you are already strong, by marking them with a star (★). (Two of them, inquiry and self-differentiation, have a bit more description at the end of this chart.)

Skill or attribute	Strong ★
1. Emotional self-regulation (I modify my emotions and thoughts, while in conversation, to remain productive.)	
2. Balance of advocating my views with inquiry* (I express my views confidently and I show genuine curiosity about other's views.)	
3. Empathy (I am good at understanding others' feelings or perspectives.)	
4. Problem-solving skills and process	
5. Being fully present, tuning out distractions	
6. Genuine listening (not just waiting to respond)	
7. Growth orientation (I seek learning over defensiveness and proving I'm right.)	
8. Self-aware (I can tune in to the assumptions and values I bring into conversations.)	
9. Adaptable thinking (I am open to embrace new viewpoints and styles.)	
10. Paraphrase (I seek clarity about what's being said by repeating what I think I heard.)	
11. Application of conflict management skills	

12. Self-differentiation* (I maintain a sense of my identity, thoughts, emotions, and values even during intense interactions.)	
13. Developmental (I build on what is already working with a conversation partner.)	
14. Clear on intentions (I know *why* I'm having the dialogue.)	
15. Known for using constructive language	
16. Anchored in organizational perspective and values (not personal grievance or biases)	
17. High attunement (I'm in touch with others' body, facial and emotional messages.)	
18. Direct and candid (I am courageous enough to speak the truth, honesty, directly and with care, as needed.)	
19. Comfortably confident (as distinct from arrogance and stubbornness)	

Now ask yourself: Which of the above 2-3 items should I target to add more skill and savvy to my work conversations? Put their numbers here: ____ ____ ____

Inquiry skill—*practicing curiosity using quality questions.* Embracing a habit of inquiry by coupling thoughtful questions with genuine interest and deep listening, is a game changer in conversations and your overall leadership. Quality inquiry prompts people to think and discover—to dig into their reservoir of creativity. It also helps others feel heard.

Here are some **powerful questions** that demonstrate inquiry with the intent to move forward effectively:

- *What would it take to create the change we need on this issue?*
- *How can I support you in taking the next step?*
- *What opportunities can you see in this?*
- *Where are we both in agreement, and what isn't clear yet for us?*
- *Can you share more about your reasoning behind your suggestion?*
- *What are we not considering in this approach?*
- *Your issue sounds complicated. How might you go about addressing it?*
- *How can we think differently about this?*
- *What challenges might come our way if we follow this course, and how do we meet them?*
- *What do you see as the best approach to addressing this issue?*

It's said that **the lack of curiosity and the drive to prove that one is *the* expert is the greatest challenge for leaders in their conversations.**[18] So, expect that for each critical conversation, there are your and other's perspectives, and reasoning behind the issue and a person's actions. Being curious helps you discover these and move towards a joint resolution.

Self-differentiation* is a psychological state[19] related to the ability to distinguish your thoughts, identity, and feelings from those of others. Why does this

---

[18] Hope. S. and Cosgrove, E. (3/10/2018). Enhancing workplace leadership conversations. www.theconversationspace.com

[19] O'Neill, M. B. 2000. Executive Coaching with Backbone and Heart: A Systems Approach to Engaging Leaders with Their Challenges, p. 19.

matter? Too often, when in conversations that create anxiety or fear, a leader may lose their grounding and become reactive. Mary Beth O'Neill describes this as *"when we lose our balance internally and respond in an automatic ineffective way."*

When you are self-differentiated, you are clear on where you stand and the reasoning behind that stance; simultaneously, you are able to interact in a way that preserves a healthy, working relationship. You experience an equilibrium, or "the *ability to maintain yourself and your relationships while pulled by the forces of fear, conflict, and anxiety.*" (O'Neill)

Here are two instances of lost self-differentiation:

- During a conflict when values collide, and you cave in (when you know you shouldn't) rather than behave assertively and respectfully.

- When setting expectations or boundaries and it's difficult for you to maintain candor when a staffer disagrees on a non-negotiable.

Consider a leader who tended to acquiesce and lose his will each time he provided developmental feedback to an often aggressive, defensive staffer. He knew he should have held him accountable, yet anxiety about the potential negative response kept the leader from standing on his values and what's best overall. He, during coaching, explored the reasoning for the feedback he was offering, and then worked to approach it differently in their next meeting. In speaking with the leader a few weeks after standing on his principles, he remarked: *"A lot of what I tolerated months ago, I am now more comfortable speaking up about without anxiety because it's the right thing for our work and our culture."* He restored equilibrium.

Adapting for style preferences. Skilled leaders are attentive to discerning what works best in light of the other conversation partner's style preferences. Building quality relationships and synergistic teams is advanced by spending time getting to know what makes others' tick. Try to uncover others' motivational factors to help bring out their best.

> *How you prefer to move through the world and engage with others is not universal. One size doesn't fit all.*

Keep this in mind: How you prefer to move through the world is not universal. What motivates you or what deflates your energy is not one-size-fits-all.

Many leaders are high energy, fast-paced, quick decision-makers, risk takers, and assertive (even aggressive) communicators. This works well for some of your people, but not so much for others. So, think about the communication preferences of each individual as you prepare for your conversations.

Below, consider your direct reports, who each have one (or a combination) of these preferred styles (based on the DISC[20] model). What might that mean for how you engage or to be more flexible with them?

Persons' initials	Tendency towards...	Common preferences	I should be less or more...
	Introversion and task oriented (C)	Slower pace Detailed Accuracy Procedure-driven Careful More formal High standards	
	Introversion and people focused (S)	Slower pace Interested in people Steady, consistency Thoughtful Loyal Cooperative Conflict averse Likes certainty	
	Extroversion and task oriented (D)	Faster pace Direct Achievement Impatient Forceful Risk taking Business focused Results-oriented	
	Extroversion and people focused (I)	Faster pace Energetic Verbalizes Social Emotional Optimistic Chatty Being accepted	

Which of these styles is the most challenging for you and why? _____

_____

_____

[20] TTI Success Insights LTD

With these conversation partners, consider their preferences (refer to the above chart or your own observations). What are 1-2 ways you can specifically adapt your approach to help achieve meaningful outcomes with them? _____

_____

_____

Practice being more expansive (adaptable) so as not to force people to always "dance to your music." People bring many and varied complementary attributes to work, and it's your job to engage in ways that leverage these talents rather than treat them as antithetical to your work.

Triggers and emotions. Sometimes we lose balance when certain events occur. Triggers are those actions, events, or situations that cause you to behave outside of your normal patterns and in ineffective ways. They cause you to veer from your normal reasonable course.

For instance, one leader's coaching goal was to demonstrate better composure and an elevated public demeanor (i.e., *presence*). He tended to yell at his staffers when frustrated. In a moment of insight, he remarked: *"I'm always talking about my staff frustrating me, but instead I should be looking at what it is about me that leads me to become frustrated in certain situations."* As he investigated his frustration triggers, he realized it happened mostly when he hadn't figured out how to develop his staffer's skills for the newly funded programs that required some different skillsets (for which there was no plan). Instead of working with them, he'd belittle them. This recognition led him to be more thoughtful in his interactions and to prioritize their skill building.

Some familiar conversation triggers. Think about the triggers that take you off your course during conversations using the list below.

1. When people don't agree with you
2. Being questioned about your logic
3. When winning matters too much
4. When self-identity, motives, values, or beliefs are questioned
5. Being accused of something
6. When you don't feel your voice is being heard
7. Situations that make you feel you have no control
8. Situations that remind you of past negative experiences
9. Statements that make you feel not valued
10. When you don't have all the answers and feel this is somehow a threat

Many of these triggers are about identity, our very sense of who we are.

"This is the conversation we each have with ourselves... we conduct an internal debate over whether this means we are competent or incompetent, a good person or bad...What impact might it have on our self-image and self-esteem,

What triggers us to emotionally derail in conversations often has to do with our identity, how we see ourselves.

our future, and our well-being?"[21]

Responses when triggered. This is where the trouble occurs. Once the trigger happens, we have a choice in our responses. If we haven't retrained our brains to regain balance, we typically respond in non-helpful ways, wherein we lose internal balance. Do you see yourself in any of the responses in the list below? Which one/s? _____

_____

1. Talk louder
2. Cut people off
3. Withdraw
4. Become angry
5. Belittle the person
6. Engage in a battle of wills
7. Lose control of logic in your thinking
8. Draw unverified conclusions
9. Become highly defensive
10. Overly argumentative
11. Over-talking, stop listening
12. Justify one's perspective by any means

Mitigating the effects when you feel triggered

In these situations, we can start by asking ourselves: *How else can I respond? What's a better way?*

Expand your range of responses: As we grow and reflect, we realize our current range of responses is limited and limiting. We explore other response options that might open the way for better results.

---

[21] Stone, D, Patton, B., and Heen. S. 2010. Difficult Conversations, p. 8.

I partnered with a leader who came to this awareness, who then began experimenting with other responses. The leader felt increased satisfaction by practicing calmness, increasing listening, and breathing deeply rather than his typical blurting out harsh words.

Pause: One often mentioned strategy when triggered is to exercise restraint by **widening the reaction time between the trigger (stimulus) and your response.** PAUSE for a minute, a day, a week. This gives you time to regain balance, restore your power to choose a better response, and tap into your capabilities that might have become blocked during stress.

Prepare: When you know you have a challenging conversation coming up, and you are aware of what might trigger you, plan ahead and identify ways to maintain your composure and focus.

Reset: Pay attention to your reactions and pull yourself back to your center, alter how you are engaging, slow your breathing to return your frame of mind back to your intent on a meaningful outcome.

Your approach: Take a moment now to think about what you can do to soften the effects and regain your emotional balance when you feel triggered.

I can _____

_____

My listening quotient

"I thought that because I was articulate, I was also good in conversations. But that's

absolutely not true. Being a good talker doesn't make you a good listener, and being smart might make you a terrible listener."[22]

While truly listening to our employees and colleagues tends to strengthen bonds, deepen engagement, and improve performance, for many leaders, listening, as in *really* listening, is extremely tedious.

"Listening is an intentional activity that requires empathy, patience, and an ability to respond to what you hear. And because it can be mentally taxing, particularly when the subject matter is complex or emotionally charged, people often take shortcuts or disengage altogether."[23]

Leaders are loaded with answers, we think quickly; after all, we tell ourselves, we have other things to do with our time. Yet, reported in one analysis: *"Listening is ranked as the most important oral communication skill in the workplace."*[24] The same publication indicates it's not only a trainable skill but one that's considered a game-changer for leaders.

"In a healthy conversation, you're present. You are listening to what's being said at that moment. If you're letting a thought distract you or if you're focused on what you want to say next, you're not listening."[25]

---

[22] Headlee, C. 2017. We Need to Talk: How to Have Conversations That Matter, p. 36

[23] Yip, J. and Fisher, C. M. Are you really a good listener. Harvard Business Review, May-June 2025.

[24] Schifrin, D. 4 Listening skills leaders need to master. Harvard Business Review, Dec. 16, 2024.

[25] Headley, C. 2017. We Need to Talk, p. 201

Pay attention to your listening habits and identify which of the following you need to develop to be more effective, relational, and productive in conversation.

- Minimize distractions to be fully "there."

- Refrain from "rehearsing," your response.

- Talk less so you can listen more. Deliberately reduce your speaking time to grant it to the other person, especially your team members.

- Pay attention to messages being sent through your partner's tone and mood.

- Use body language that indicates receptivity, (e.g., eye contact, relaxed posture, nodding to affirm understanding, etc.)

- Validate the other's thoughts as they share.

- Get comfortable with a bit of silence; it allows people time to process their thoughts.

- Ask meaningful questions to prompt the other person's thinking, rather than constantly offering your solutions.

- Paraphrase to be sure you grasp the person's point ..." It sounds (or "I think I hear you saying"), "Is that right?"

- Take mental notes of the partner's stories so you can recall them later (builds rapport).

- Keep yourself open to others' thoughts.

- Refrain from interrupting or talking over the other person. This helps you delay offering solutions before fully grasping their issue.

○ Limit telling your similar story; let your
   employees have their time.

In summary, **balance the conversation's content and
the relationship,** since the quality of the relationship
often determines how people respond to the subject
matter. If, for example, you get a defensive response
to your challenging feedback, you can remind the
person that your goal is to support them in doing their
work. If, on the other hand, you are hyper focused on
their comfort, you might need to keep the issues
upfront with clarity, candor, and seriousness.

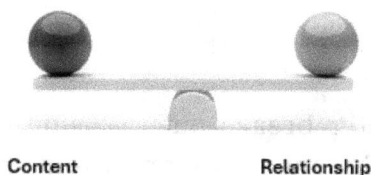

Content   Relationship

Action: One immediate change goes a long way

Name one change you will make in your conversation
quality that can help you achieve better effects.

My one change: _____

This ends Chapter 3, which offered you a chance to
examine your current and desired conversation
habits, processes, and quality. Next, we will look at
processes and conversation models to support you.

Chapter 4

Better Conversations; A Purposeful, Powerful and Pivotal Process

This chapter breaks out two simple but powerful frameworks, one for <u>planning</u> and one for <u>executing</u> purposeful conversations that prompt action and foster healthy relationships. Both general structures, once internalized, can be adapted as situations arise.

> *"Taking time to improve our conversations is probably one of the best ways we can spend our time because so much of our success and happiness hinge on how well we communicate."*[26]

The hallmarks of better conversations are planning, presence, purpose, meaningful questions, attentive listening, and actionable agreements.

---

[26] Knight, J. 2016. Better Conversations: Coaching Ourselves and Each Other to Be More Credible, Caring, and Connected, p. 3.

So, I repeat (from page 13): Before every IMPORTANT conversation, take at least a few minutes to answer the following six questions.

A conversation PLANNING thought process

1. **WHY** am I having this conversation?

2. **WHAT** are the best outcomes I want from this conversation (for me AND my conversation partner)?

3. What **INFORMATION** am I using that makes this conversation important? Is it factual, hearsay, an assumption, a feeling?

4. **HOW** should I structure it to make the best use of the time allotted?

5. At the end of the meeting, what **RESULTS** or next steps do I want to leave with?

6. **SELF-MANAGEMENT**: How will I situate myself - my emotions, body, and voice - to bring my best to the conversation?

In time, you will be able to answer these questions almost instinctively, though some thoughtfulness and information-gathering are essential. Here's a little bit more explanation.

Q1. WHY am I having this conversation? *What type of conversation am I having? (See sample list in Chapter 5)? What is the issue, opportunity, or challenge? What do I want to accomplish? Do I really need to have it? What's at stake for the individual, others, or the organization? How will I frame it?*

Conversation framing is critical in that it sets the stage by contextualizing it. You mentally clarify the perspective you are taking related to the work, team, or organization. You should be able to state the issue or opportunity clearly and succinctly, so it doesn't get lost. *Name the issue.*

Q2: WHAT are the ideal outcomes I want from this conversation for me AND my conversation partner? *What might be some shared goals? What are we already aligned on? Are there any non-negotiables I will need to stand on?* (Make a brief list of desired outcomes for you and the other person as well.)

Q3: WHAT information am I using that makes this conversation important? *Is it factual information, hearsay, an assumption, a feeling? Do I have the right information? Do I have relevant, useful examples?*

Q4: HOW should I plan to make the best use of the time allotted? *What is my sample flow/agenda for the* *topic?* (Remember, it may not necessarily follow the order you planned, so make sure you remain flexible). Also ask yourself: *How much time will I dedicate to this conversation?* (15, 30 60 minutes?)

Q5: At the end of the meeting, what RESULTS or next steps do I think we should leave with? *Are there actions, agreements, tangible items to leave with? How will I wrap things up, so we are both clear on our next steps? How do I envision both of us feeling at the end?*

Q6: SELF-MANAGEMENT: How will I situate myself to bring my best to the conversation? (Consider your past habits, emotions, or biases that proved not helpful and possibly caused the conversation to get off track? *What triggers me sometimes, and how will I manage my responses? How do I remain open and curious about their perspectives on the issue? Do I need to listen more and talk less or relax myself? Do I drag on too long?)* Make notes.

Here's an example from a frustrated mid-level leader who then applied the six-question framework to prepare for a conversation.

I want this conversation to move Janice to improve her documents, so they are error free. I want to encourage her to act and not deflate her energy, and I want her to recognize that it really does matter to her and the department. I want her to determine how to get this done with immediacy. I will stay focused and not come across intimidating during a 30-minute conversation. To manage my tendency to react with impatience or talk round and round if she says she has no time to check her documents, I will slow my breathing, ask her what she needs to do to allocate a bit more time, and figure out 1-2 ways she can carve out a few minutes for proofreading. I will let her know I am confident she can do it and be sure she understands that it is important to our department's reputation. I will follow up with her in two weeks to check in on accomplishing this.

The leader shared with me that the conversation went better than expected. The staff person wasn't very defensive and was happy the leader was trying to help her solve the work challenge. This shows that preparation and setting aside assumptions about how people will respond can improve effectiveness.

A sample conversation EXECUTION process

By now, you have probably noticed there's a significant kinship between better conversations and supervisory coaching methods. Both rely on thoughtfully framing issues, are mostly question driven, and require the leader to be an attentive, present listener with keen observation skills.

This next section offers a general structure for engaging in better, consequential conversations. Once you've decided on the type or subject of the conversation, you can apply this structure to it. Examples of various conversations, using or adapting this structure are in Chapter 5.

```
                        ┌──────────┐
                        │ Initiate/ │
                        │ Purpose   │
                        └──────────┘

      ┌───────────┐                    ┌───────────┐
      │AFTER: Follow│                   │Explore Topic│
      │   up on    │                    └───────────┘
      │ Promises   │
      └───────────┘

      ┌───────────┐                    ┌───────────┐
      │Close: Confirm│                  │Final Feedback│
      │ promises &  │                   └───────────┘
      │   dates     │
      └───────────┘
                    ┌──────────────┐
                    │ Reach Shared  │
                    │Understanding  │
                    └──────────────┘
```

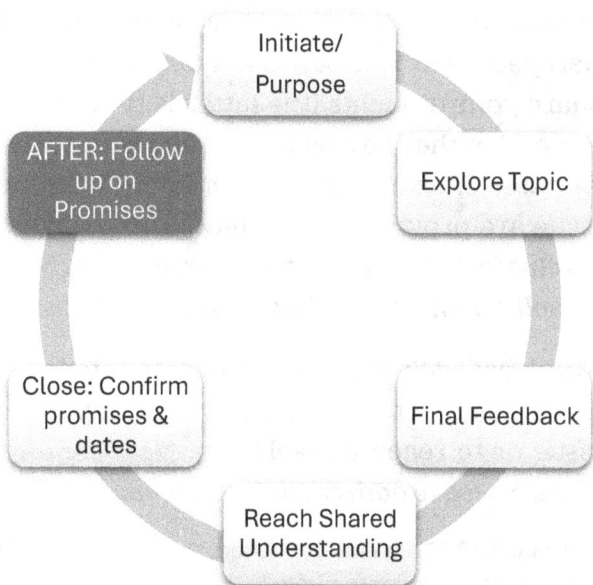

With planning *and* process, conversations can achieve better results, reduce repetitive concerns, improve connections, inspire people to deliver better work, and more effectively navigate testy terrain.

Description of the elements

Planning (i.e., preparation) was addressed in the previous pages of this chapter. You will have already done this before initiating the conversation.

1) *Initiate and Purpose.* This sets the right tone and includes a greeting, rapport-building small talk (if appropriate), and the conversation's purpose.

2) *Explore the issue(s).* This is the main part of the conversation, to explore the background and

importance of the issue, along with your and their perspectives. You can use questions as well as share your thoughts (the latter is typically better done after they have shared their perspective). (In Chapter 5, examples of questions to explore the issue are provided). *"The main thing I want us to resolve is (topic). What are your thoughts? How can we solve this? I'd like to add a few thoughts...*

3) *Final feedback.* This is a moment to offer space for anything else that might have an impact on the issue or to reach a resolution. *"Is there anything else we need to address before moving forward?"*

NOTE: Items 4 and 5 are closely related; they can be combined or spend just a few moments on Item 4.

4) *Shared understanding.* This provides a summary of the issue, the desired state, its importance and how it will be addressed. *"In summary, what we've agreed to do going forward is...xxx because xxx" (why it matters).*

5) *Closing: Promises and dates.* The conversation is not complete until you close it out. Here, you specify next steps, promises of altered attitude or actions, who is responsible and the due dates for completion. *"Let's review our next steps: What actions are you/I committed to taking and when will you/I take them?"* You also identify when the actions and follow-up will take place (as needed). Always end with a thank you for the time and the

thoughts shared. (See the next section for one liner ideas for starting and ending conversations.)

6) LATER, *Follow-up on Promises*: This is a later check-in to confirm progress on actions.

Starting and ending conversations well

Starting (Initiating)

How you initiate the conversation is key to how the rest of it goes. As already stated, it's here that you set the stage, connect as fellow humans and begin focusing on the key topics. It's short, a bit relational depending on the subject (always respectful and humane), and sets the tone. Tougher, more high-risk conversations should, within the first few minutes, start by establishing a clear purpose (or topic).

> *"We can't always control how a conversation goes, but we can create an environment for open, authentic communication by sharing our expectations and being aware of our own thoughts and feelings before we decide to speak. We can fertilize the ground before we plant the seeds."*[27]

Though it sounds simplistic, there are far too many work conversations that begin with awkwardness, *uhs, ums,* and *ahs*, no eye contact, and silent standoffs. So, starting with simple words and eye contact can get the ball rolling.

---

[27] Headlee, C. p. 56

Depending on the nature of the conversation, especially those with positive themes, you can spend a few extra minutes building rapport before launching into the business. That might be asking about the person, their family, or vacations. Even this should be short to allow time to get into the purpose of the conversation.

Look at these. Maybe one will work for you; maybe you have your own appropriate for the situation.

Good afternoon, I hope you are having a good day.	*Hello Janet, It's good to have a bit of time to talk with you.*	*Hello, thanks for this time to talk. I want us to address an important issue....*
How's your day coming along? What's on your mind?	*Hello Anika, I asked for this time for us to talk together about...*	*Good morning, how is the new project going? I'd like us to spend time on...*
Hello James, It's good to see you. Can we talk about your progress on?	*Hello there, I'd like us to get caught up on a few things.*	Yours:

Ending (Closing it out)

In contrast, many conversations end awkwardly, or they go on so long that the point is lost or the topic loses potency. Try not to exceed the time you scheduled for the conversation. **When you're done, be done.** If you can't get to the place you wanted, accept unfinished business and determine when to continue the dialogue.

Closing a conversation well and cleanly:

- Shows respect for people's time and attention.
- Brings closure, signaling "we're done."
- Enhances rapport.
- Demonstrates maturity and professionalism.

Tip: When the other person is very long-winded, wait for an opening, kindly interject, and give a neat close.

Look at these various closing phrases. Again, maybe one will work for you, or use your own.

This has been helpful. Let's wrap up and quickly recap what comes next.	*It's been an hour, and that's all I have for now. Let's pick a time to revisit this.*	*We've accomplished a lot; let's close it out. Thanks for your time.*

Let's finish up. We've probably taken this as far as we can right now.	*With respect for the time we committed, let's close out for now. Thank you.*	*That's all I have. Before we close, do you have anything else?*
We both have lots of work waiting for us, so let's stop here. Thank you.	*To wrap things up, thank you for sharing your time and your thoughts.*	Yours:

Deconstructing and reconstructing an unsatisfying conversation

Here's another and last exercise before looking at the adaptable conversation blueprints in Chapter 5.

We can all learn from our experiences even, and especially, the bad ones. In fact, the best leaders are those who are secure enough to admit when they've made mistakes. They might say to their staffer: *"Hey, I'd like to revisit our last conversation. I think I messed that one up, and I'm sorry about that."* Glaser[28] refers to this as *"examining conversations after the fact to*

---

[28] Glaser, J. E. 2014. Conversational Intelligence: How Great Leaders Build Trust and Get Extraordinary Results, p. 13.

garner new insights about them." I remind you, the aim is better, not perfection.

So, if you're having repetitive conversations with the same person (for something that really matters), de-construct and re-construct them. Try this exercise to get you closer to achieving the change you seek.

Think of a recent disappointing conversation you had. (When? With whom? About?) _____

_____

Now, respond to the items below to think through and reshape your input. Maybe it will help the next time.

Deconstruct (for reflective thinking)

1. First, examine what was actually beneficial in this "bad" conversation. What went well?

_____

2. Your triggers: What values/beliefs do you feel were challenged that set you off course? What about your partner's behavior was bothersome for you?

_____

   a. What did you say, do, or feel in response to these challenges noted in #2?

_____

   b. What was the effect on the conversation?

_____

3. What did you say or do in this conversation to affect it in a positive manner?

4. What did you say or do to affect it in an unproductive way?

5. Did you have the relevant facts, or what might have been missing that mattered to the conversation?

Reconstruct (for learning and future conversations)

6. What could you have said or done to maintain focus on the topic and preserve your emotional equilibrium?

7. What might you have said or done differently to get your point across in a way that your partner could better receive it?

8. What reminders can you give yourself for the next conversation?

9. What did you learn?

I was speaking with a massage therapist, who recounted how her previous employer had given her feedback that had included some positives, but the negatives were what rang out and haunted her for weeks, even months. She hated that conversation. She remarked: *Don't the leaders need to learn how to talk with people before they start telling people what they need to do?* Good question. So, I asked her if she were to reconstruct that conversation, what might have been said or done that would have helped her accept and act on the feedback with her self-esteem still intact. She said.... *Ask me what I think about the items she raised; that would have helped and kept my defenses down some.*

As a leader, when your conversations go off track or they feel like a cluster of wasted words and time, ask yourself: *What could I have done or said to make it more effective, achieve better results, and leave the person's self-worth intact?*

> Ask yourself, when conversations go wrong: *What could I have done or said to make it more effective and with everyone's self-worth undisturbed?*

Checklist: Before you jump right in...

For critical issues, planned conversations go better than unplanned. With a framework for the conversation set, you now have room to improvise during the "real" dialogue. Improvisation shows that you are present, can adapt, manage your emotions, and be empathetic where needed, while staying focused on the aim of the conversation. Ready?

- ☑ I know the purpose.
- ☑ I have set a time and drafted a flow for the conversation.
- ☑ I have prepared how I will start the conversation, so the topic/issue is clear and important.
- ☑ Conversations are two-way; I know conversations are two-way, so I am ready to listen genuinely and to assert my views when needed.
- ☑ I am ready to spend more time on solutions than on fixating on the past.
- ☑ I feel settled and ready to be present.
- ☑ I am ready to improvise, edit my behavior, even after I've planned since "scripts are not enough."
- ☑ I am aware there may be more than "my story" at work in the situation.
- ☑ The outcome and the connection are important aims; I will strive to balance them.
- ☑ I don't have to be right; I strive for good joint results.
- ☑ If there are non-negotiables, I am clear on them and will maintain them.
- ☑ Ultimately, I am aiming for a quality conversation that achieves results and reduces the need to have the same conversation repeatedly.

My Conversation Profile: A Summary

Before planning your high-stakes conversations, summarize your conversation habits here and refer to this when using the conversations templates.

Reviewing Chapter 3 might help you complete this.

1. These are my positive attributes, tendencies, and patterns during conversations:

----

2. These are my unproductive conversations habits:

----

3. These are the typical trigger situations that could throw me off during conversations:

----

4. These are strategies I need to use to manage myself when I feel stress during conversations:

My Conversation Profile: A Summary

Here's a sample based on one client's patterns.

1. **My positive attributes, tendencies, and patterns during conversations:**
   Asking clarifying and probing questions, caring demeanor, listening, genuine desire to understand the other perspective, open to talking to everyone.

2. **My unproductive conversations habits:**
   Worry about not being liked if providing critical feedback, change tone and words to soften things, overexplain, impatient with "lazy" people, not coming to a clear summary of next steps at end of the conversation, passive-aggressive language

3. **These are the typical trigger situations that could throw me off during conversations:**
   Comments that seem to be belittling my identity as a woman and/or African American, comments that seem to say I don't know what I'm talking about, diminishing my role/status with common language, like calling me "girl" at work, things I perceive as disrespectful

4. **These are strategies I need to use to manage myself when I feel stress during conversations:**
   Do self-talk to calm myself down, practice focusing, use calm/pleasant facial expressions, prepare my thoughts and attitude to be open to multiple options, say something reassuring to the other person, breathe before responding, remember to stop talking so much, end by wrapping up and clarifying next steps

Your Adaptable Conversation Guides

❖ **Which conversation are you having?**

Choose the guide in this chapter and adapt it to your style and situation.

10 conversation guides:

- Goal setting
- Under-performance
- Setting new priorities and direction
- One on One meetings (various situations)
- Build or repair a relationship (new, ongoing, strained, repair)
- Career advancement (e.g., promotion, raises, retention)
- Poor interaction patterns
- Performance checkpoints
- Valued contributions feedback
- Team meetings or conversations (various including mediating conflicts)

Chapter 5

Adaptable Conversations Guides

This "how-to" chapter is one you will use repeatedly as you address your most crucial work conversations.

> *"Conversation is the pathway that we as humans use to pursue all of the things that we want to achieve...As a manager, as a leader, as a group, as a department, as an organization, whatever goals you have, you are going to have to **talk to people** to achieve them."*[29]

What follows are examples, not scripts, since conversations are alive with human emotions and not fully predictable. Each guide has an introduction, tips, sample format, and questions that may stimulate reflective thinking. A planning worksheet is also included. Most of these conversations can follow the structure outlined in Chapter 4.

---

[29] Brooks, A. W., 2025. TALK: The Science of Conversation and the Art of Being Ourselves. Accessed at: www.charterworks.com/talk-brooks-full/

Four suggestions before using the guides

When using one of these conversation guides, these suggestions are key to success:

1. Do not use verbatim! Review them, select what you can use in your situations, edit, and make it your own.

2. Do not use all of the suggested questions included with each conversation guide. The intent is to help you make it a conversation by inserting some questions. Select one, two or your own that fit the situation and are stated in your voice and words.

3. Put the conversation in your voice and words.

4. Some conversations will have more or less than you need, so do not feel compelled to use all the items in the guide.

1. GOAL SETTING

The annual goal setting conversation with your direct reports is an excellent time to accomplish several things. You can express the value of their work, re-connect their work and goals to the organization's existing or new priorities, hear their thoughts on goals they believe would add value, increase your learning about their work, draft and agree on their goals, and strengthen your partnership.

Situations: Annual or new hire

Ideally, the staffer and the supervising manager co-create the goals aligned with the business priorities.

Tips:

✓ Include goals for professional, measurable job accomplishments <u>and</u> for professional growth and development (i.e., soft skills).

✓ It may take two sessions to finalize. The aim in the first is to draft the goals; the second, after reviewing and editing, is to finalize the goals.

✓ This is also an opportunity to garner input on frequency and structure of their one-on-one meetings and topics for team meetings.

Suggested goal setting preparation:

1. Determine how much time you will devote to this.

2. Ask the staffer to prepare and bring the following:

   ☐ Three to five (3-5) items they believe should be the highest priorities for their annual goals

   ☐ Suggestions for their next year's technical and soft skills development, along with the rationale

   ☐ Their thoughts on a) career aspirations and pathway, and 2) work satisfaction

3. Your preparation:

   ☐ Prepare a draft of objectives you'd like included (consider additions or exclusion from prior year goals), ideas for professional and interpersonal growth to take their work to the next level.

   ☐ Have the organizational priorities available, especially the parts related to your team's work. This helps staff see the alignment and rationale behind their next year's goals and objectives.

Possible questions during goalsetting: (options)

If there is one area where you know you could far exceed expectations what would that be?

What thoughts do you have about how the goals contribute to the organization's priorities?

What specific goals or work results matter most to you?

What learning opportunities would you like to pursue to enhance your work?

Look at this flow and sample dialogue. Adapt it to meet your needs.

1.	Open by thanking them for their work the previous year and how it contributed to the goals.	*It's good to have this time to sit together to set goals for the upcoming year. First, I want to thank you for your contributions last year. They helped us achieve the department's goals in support of the organization's strategic objectives.* (If you have details on this, share briefly.)
2.	Review the current organizational goals that their work is tied to. Share what excites you about these goals or their importance.	*I realize there's a lot we could prioritize, so let's review the top priorities for our team to help draft your annual goals. First, are you clear how our team's work fits into the organization's goals?* Leave a moment for a response. *I'm excited about it and how each of us plays a significant part.*
3.	Review direct report's suggested goals.	*Let's start with the list you prepared, then I'll share mine and see how we can align them to achieve the new priorities, engage the best of your strengths, adjust any work tasks based on new priorities, and ensure the goals are a stretch and achievable without overburdening your job.*

4.	Sharing... theirs and yours	Allow time to share theirs and listen for alignment as you then share yours.
5.	Where do we already have alignment?	*Let's confirm where we are already aligned with new goals.* What's aligned helps get some of the goals established.
6.	Where are we not aligned?	*Let's look at where we aren't fully aligned. I can share, based on our priorities, which goals are required (non-negotiable) and then we can go from there.* Allow staffer to respond.
7.	Agree on the work goals for a draft	Review the agreed upon goals and seek buy in for any non-negotiables by sharing the reasoning for these goals.
8.	Draft some professional development goals	*Let's spend a bit of time talking about career development, your hopes, and interests. These goals address how you would like to grow your leadership skills and attributes and how we might structure that learning this year.* . *You prepared some thoughts, so let's go through those. Then I might have some ideas on possible growth targets this year as well.* (If they covered this well, there is no need for you to add.)

9. Begin making them actionable and measurable	*Can we review the goals to be sure we have clarity on the actions and measures for them? Let's look at the SMART framework to do that. We can each work on this afterwards before we finalize them since it may take some thought and time to flesh out.*
10. Wrap Up and Next Steps	*This has been helpful. Next, we need to sharpen the goals,* confirm changes, and finalize. (State who does what and when). *As we wrap up, let me ask you:* 1) *Are there any potential barriers that might interfere with achieving these? How can we overcome them?* 2) *Is there anything else you will need to bring your best to achieving these goals?* 3) *Can you clearly see your vital role in helping the team achieve the impact we seek to make?* Offer any known resources to support the employees success. Close on a positive note.

SMART Framework for Writing Goals

Many organizations use the SMART framework for goal setting; some use other methods. The advantage of this framework is that it brings clarity for both the manager and staff person and reduces the chances of subjectivity or bias during the year-end evaluation. It also removes confusion about what success looks like because it's clear and measurable. Staffers can see where they are along the way and, if circumstances dictate change, you can amend the goals to improve or change their expected performance.

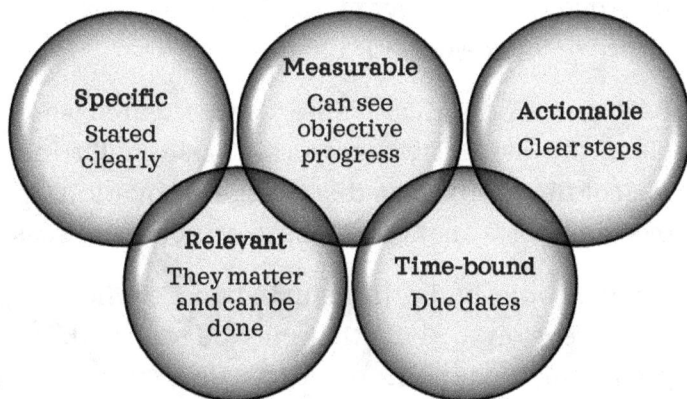

Example 1: *As team manager, I will strengthen cross departmental collaboration and collegiality by identifying, planning, and executing two strategic projects over the next six months between my team and a team that has an impact on the results. To accomplish this, my team members will get training to enhance their communication and collaboration skills.*

This is **specific** (build collegial, cross-collaboration), **measurable** (two successful projects), **achievable** (especially with some training), **relevant** (strategic projects), **time bound** (six months).

Example 2: *Within 120 days, I will ensure all approved invoices are being paid within 30 days of approved submission, utilizing more efficient, user-friendly systems and staff training and effective prioritizing.*

It's **specific** (pay approved invoices within 30 days), **measurable** (all are paid unless extenuating circumstances arise), **achievable** (with process improvements), **relevant** (satisfaction and reputation improves), **time bound** (120 days).

Be aware of the disadvantages that can arise when using the SMART framework. Those might include lack of flexibility, may discourage innovation, and an overemphasis on the metrics may increase stress.

Goals should be both inspiring and challenging, so pay attention to goals that may be too rigid. During your goal checkpoint meetings, determine whether they need to be modified to meet the needs of the organization and the staff person.

Closing thought: Transform your goal setting sessions into productive, affirming, and high-performance focused engagements. These can also strengthen manager/employee trust and collaboration.

Plan and Practice Worksheet

What's the conversation topic? _____

Who is your conversation with? _____

Why does it matter to have this conversation and now?

_____

_____

1) How much time will you set for the conversation?
   15 minutes ○ 30 minutes ○ an hour ○ other: ○

2) Where will you have it? _____

3) What information will be used for this conversation?

4) What are the best outcomes for both you and your
   conversation partner? What should be clear

5) What could possibly make the conversation go off
   track, and how might you respond if that happens?

6) What are some reminders to yourself to help you
   manage yourself well?
   a.
   b.

7) What's an effective way to open (*initiate*) the conversation?

8) What is a possible flow (agenda) for the conversation (to *clarify purpose and explore the issue*)?

a.

b.

c.

d.

e.

f.

9) Agreements (*promises*): Be sure to end with agreements and clear, specific next steps. (Identify during the meeting and make note of them here)

Action	By whom?	By when?

10) What will be your approach to closing/wrapping up the conversation (i.e., ending well)? _____
_____

2. UNDER-PERFORMANCE

Underperformance describes a situation in which an employee is falling short of their job expectations. The skilled leader addresses less-than-optimal work output long before the annual review to provide the staffer with an opportunity and support to raise their level of accomplishment. When managed well, many employees actually improve their work. Offering quality, honest feedback is a powerful driver for achieving better results.

Ignoring underperformance can adversely affect productivity, team morale, and work quality. It also sends a message that low performance is tolerated and that you don't have high expectations for the work or the quality of your team's work culture.

Situations: Staff person not meeting the expected job goals; when the wrong work is being done, when behavioral standards are transgressed affecting the work culture and productivity.

Examples: consistently not meeting milestones, repeated mistakes, frequent absences, chronic lateness (on tasks or attendance), lackluster energy, disrupting teamwork, not adapting to new processes or standards, disregarding policies, negativity.

Tips:

✓ Think of this as a process: 1) Assess, 2) provide feedback, 3) plan for positive change, and 4) monitor progress together.

✓ Don't delay. Early intervention allows time to provide any performance support needed.

✓ Don't overload with criticism. Focus on the areas of concern that matter most.

✓ Be open to learn more about the situation the staffer might be facing; being receptive to explore some "could be" causes.

✓ Accept there may be organizational barriers to staff achieving the required work results. Look at the factors below and be ready to address any that have a bearing on improving your staffer's performance.

☐ unclear job expectations
☐ work overload
☐ temporary personal concerns (e.g., health or stressors)
☐ competing priorities that take time away from core performance goals
☐ insufficient knowledge or skills (can these be provided?)
☐ missing the right tools and resources
☐ lacking the needed cooperation, teamwork, or coordination to get the job done
☐ poor incentive system or the wrong work is incentivized
☐ lack of ongoing quality feedback and coaching

Some underperformance preparation items:

☐ Ask your direct report to write brief notes for the meeting addressing the areas where they are not meeting goals so far. Include a) their reasoning for being behind on the goals, b) what they will do to improve on the goals, sufficient to achieve the expectations, and c) identify any reasonable support that would help them achieve their goals.

☐ Your preparation: a) schedule a good time and place, b) review the goals that are, to date, being underperformed and be able to state it clearly, and c) set your mind and intention on prompting improvement, not castigating, deflating or threatening termination (unless this is chronic, which requires a process involving your human resources department.)

☐ Reflect on and determine any shortcomings you need to address to evoke better outcomes, e.g., sharpen goal clarity, remove low priority tasks, schedule regular coaching, find deficiency-related learning opportunities.

Possible questions (options):

How would you describe your performance on the specific goals where you seem to be falling short?

What would you need to not only achieve your goals but also find the tasks highly satisfying?

What are your expectations and aspirations for your goals overall by yearend?

Is there anything about these goals that we need to think about together?

Are there practical things I can address that will make it possible for you to achieve these goals?

Look at this flow and sample dialogue. Adapt it or use it for ideas to structure your conversation.

1.	Initiate the conversation and state the topic	*Hello xxx. I'd like us to use this time to talk about some of your work milestones that appear to be falling short of expectations. Before we end, I want to determine the actions you will take to meet expectations and how I can support you in doing so.*
2.	Explore the areas of concern	*Let's start by having you go through what you prepared to address your current shortfalls and suggestions to bring your work up to the level needed.* Listen intently while they go through what they've prepared; only interject if you need clarity on what they are saying.

2a. Sharing your views for alignment	If what they shared sounds great, confirm it works and ask whether they need anything from you to help achieve the goals in a timely, quality manner. If they missed anything that seems important, you might say: *Thanks for thinking through the items and proactively offering strategies to improve. I would like to be clear about what else is important and how I came to see things this way.* (Share that.)
3. Final feedback	*Is there anything we've missed?* Or *Are there other thoughts we need to share before moving forward?*
4. Shared understanding on agreements	*For clarity, let's review what will happen next for you to get up to speed on your performance and set a specific timeline.* (Review actions on improvement and follow-up after the meeting with an email confirmation.)
5. Wrap Up and Next Steps	*This has been helpful, and I am pleased to have you continue supporting the goals and achieving success in your role. Your work matters to our collective success.*

As we wrap up, I'd like us to check-in on progress on these action steps in a month. Does that work for you? Finally: *I have agreed to support you by doing what you've identified including xxx and* (if you have other ideas, offer any known resources to support the employees success.) Close session on a respectful note.

Closing thought: Strive to turn these often-avoided, anxiety-producing conversations into engagements that set the staffer on a course to improved performance. To do so, be clear, supportive, encouraging, and honest; install accountability processes that are regular; acknowledge progress; and foster continued improvements. Since this is often a tenuous or avoided conversation, spend time before the conversation on the worksheet provided on the next page.

Plan and Practice Worksheet

What's the conversation topic? _____

Who is your conversation with? _____

Why does it matter to have this conversation and now?

_____

_____

1) How much time will you set for the conversation?
   15 minutes○ 30 minutes ○ an hour ○ other: ○

2) Where will you have it? _____

3) What information will be used for this conversation?

4) What are the best outcomes for both you and your
   conversation partner? What should be clear

5) What could possibly make the conversation go off
   track, and how might you respond if that happens?

6) What are some reminders to yourself to help you
   manage yourself well?
   a.
   b.

7) What's an effective way to open (*initiate*) the conversation?

8) What is a possible flow (agenda) for the conversation (to *clarify purpose and explore the issue*)?

a.

b.

c.

d.

e.

f.

9) Agreements (*promises*): Be sure to end with agreements and clear, specific next steps. (Identify during the meeting and make note of them here)

Action	By whom?	By when?

10) What will be your approach to closing/wrapping up the conversation (i.e., ending well)? _____
_____

3. SET NEW PRIORITIES/DIRECTION

Inevitably the organization's priorities will change, or new initiatives will be implemented to ensure the organization remains both responsive to their customers' evolving needs and financially viable. Launching these new or altered priorities well is important and should include a conversation with your team, rather than just a declaration.

New priorities will likely affect everyone's work to some degree. So, conversations might be in order with your team and each direct report. This is a chance to create clarity, inspire action, identify new learning initiatives, and enhance commitment. Done well, you can achieve all of these. Done poorly, you may face sentiments such as confusion, grumbling, unfocused work, or diminished motivation.

Situations: New strategic plan priorities or shifting job priorities, when decisions dramatically change work tasks, when launching new team initiatives

Tips:

✓ Amplify the potential positives that can emerge from the new direction or when the staff's job segments are changed or reprioritized.

✓ Know that people may not immediately embrace the changes. Don't be surprised at the range of emotions and attitudes that might show up (e.g., fear, openness, sadness, resistance, indifference, excitement). So, breathe and help them process.

✓ Plan to share the new direction and priorities and leave space for people to get clarity and begin exploring the implications for their work and how to move forward constructively and productively.

✓ Speak about the changes in your voice. ("We are moving in this direction" rather than "they said").

Preparation suggestions:

☐ Be clear and informed about the rationale for the new priorities and how they affect the team; have a written summary of them.

☐ A few days in before the meeting, share the new priorities document and a short agenda for the meeting. (Use or adapt the sample [p. 102] to create an agenda).

☐ Determine whether you will plan for an hour (to introduce, review the priorities, and begin strategizing on how the team's work will look), or a longer summit (half or full day) to flesh out the changes more fully.

☐ Anticipate questions your team might have about the changes and their effect on them; pre-think your responses but remain flexible.

☐ Determine, in advance, the tone you want to set, how you hope the staffers will feel by the close of the conversation, and how you might shape the conversation to achieve that.

☐ Prepare some thought-provoking questions that allow the team to talk and think about the future related to these changes.

Possible questions (options):

How might these decisions help you make even more valuable contributions to the work?

How have you tended to respond to changes that you didn't initiate? Give an example.

In this situation, what options would you recommend for moving forward?

What is not clear to you right now? How can we make it clearer?

What is a way to look at these changes in the most positive light?

What will we need to know, learn, and do to implement these changes with high effectiveness?

Look at the following sample meeting dialogue. Adapt it or use it for ideas to meet your needs.

1. Initiate the conversation and state the topic	*I appreciate everyone joining this conversation to explore the new priorities and how we will reframe what success looks like for our team.*

		(Depending on the weightiness and meeting time allocated, you might start with a warm-up activity, e.g., a quote about change, a round robin question, or with voluntary sharing on *"me and change"*... *one positive change that happened recently and how I reacted, and one change I didn't welcome initially and how I reacted.*
2.	Review the new priorities	Go through the new priorities and reinforce the team's valuable role in achieving them. *Before exploring these further, are there any questions about how they are stated or the rationale for these changes?* (Offer just a few minutes and maybe just make note of the questions if not answered easily; don't let this drag because you will spend time during the next part of the agenda on prompting them to think about the new priorities.)
3.	Explore the new priorities	Break into small groups and have them respond to these four questions: (maybe use 15 minutes of a 60-minute meeting or more time in a longer session.) 1. *How can you envision these priorities having a positive effect on the organization?*

	2. *What adjustments will our team need to make to help achieve these new priorities?* 3. *Is there anything that requires more clarity before we move forward?* 4. *What three best next steps do you suggest the team take to begin moving forward?* Each group should summarize the responses and be ready to share with everyone. Have each group share their summaries in 2-3 minutes (give more time if this is a longer meeting). Then compile the items, give time for any comments, and determine the next best steps, based on the top items identified. Review them aloud and confirm the steps are corrected stated.
5. Share leader's thoughts and words of confidence	Assuming the group did a decent job, thank them for their insightful thinking on realigning their work for the new priorities. If you have thoughts to add or if there was anything raised that is not negotiable, identify those items and the reasoning.

		Finally, express confidence in moving forward and excitement about the team's vital role in achieving these new goals.
6.	Final shared understanding	*Before we close, let's be sure we've covered all we should for now. Let me ask: Is there anything right now that's unsaid but important to understanding and beginning to plan for these new priorities?*
7.	Agreements/ Next Steps	*This has been a beneficial use of our time, allowing us to move in the same direction and start with some initial next steps.* Review the next steps and who will be responsible for each one.
		Close meeting on a positive note.

Special situation: *Unpopular decisions staffers may not like (not termination).*

This is specifically related to changes in how staffers will need to reallocate their time and resources for different tasks. It likely means less or no emphasis on work tasks they are accustomed to doing. When changes occur in the priorities, you may be thinking: *"I need Jeremy to let go of spending time on managing the mentorship project and prioritize recruitment; I don't think he'll like that."* Or *"I'm going to have to let the team know the budget will no longer allow us to have our offsite retreats or use PTO for volunteer service."*

What should these conversations look like? Given all that's involved in coming to an informed, major decision, delivering the news to the impacted staffers likely will require planning and finesse.

Possible questions:

What's not fully clear to you about this decision?

How can this decision be a driver for us to deliver outstanding work?

What challenges might come our way, and how can we overcome them?

What needs to be true for this to work?

How do we keep our energy and commitment high in light of these changes?

Use the meeting format provided on the previous pages, while remaining cognizant of productively managing the possible staff's emotional load.

Closing thought: Keep in mind that having well-planned and executed conversations with staff about new priorities goes a long way. They offer space for clarity about the expectations and the reasoning behind them, opportunities for those affected to share their thoughts and feel heard, alleviate anxiety, and set the course for recalibrating the work in a healthy, informed way.

4. ONE-ON-ONE MEETINGS

One of the most essential functions of a supervisory leader is establishing and maintaining a rhythm of planned and purposeful time with each direct report. These one-on-one meetings are special moments that can achieve several goals at once. Staffers have reported these private conversations with their manager help them: *sustain work motivation, maintain high job achievements, feel heard and valued, be accountable to work standards, develop new skills and improve mindset, understand their role, improve receptivity to change and feedback, and stay with the organization over an extended period.* For the leader, some benefits that accrue are: *gain a partner to co-create processes and approaches to the work, access more ideas on leading the team, build rapport, and help deepen staff engagement.*

When these conversations aren't prioritized or given attention, either owing to infrequency, haphazard planning, or when approached as a rote "have to do," engagement and performance will likely suffer.

***Situations*:** Regular, supervisory meetings with individual direct reports; you can also address other topics such as project design, career development, work climate, employee satisfaction, recognition, intention to stay, performance planning, input on team needs, say "No" or delay approving a request.

Tips:

✓ Determine a regular one-on-one meeting rhythm with each direct report (weekly or bi-monthly are the most common; new hires profit from greater frequency until they learn their roles).

✓ At the start of each year, ask each direct report what they want out of the one-on-ones, topics they want to address, ideas for team meeting topics, and confirm the rhythm and length of meetings.

✓ Strike a good balance between work updates (or project status) and developmental topics.

✓ Establish rapport with each direct report. This helps them feel they can trust you to be honest about their work, lives, and their needs.

✓ Be sure to follow through on anything you've agreed to do during the conversation.

✓ Encourage staffers to own the session content (by bringing items they want to address), while you provide the structure that culminates in some meaningful results or next steps.

✓ Take these one-on-ones seriously by prioritizing them, trying your best not to cancel. When there's a time crunch or not enough to address, you can abbreviate these personal times.

✓ Remember, these conversations help you know your people as unique humans. This allows you to help them, in their own way, think through issues and build resilience and problem-solving skills.

Preparation:

☐ Be ready to be fully present, interested, and in more of a listening than telling/advising mode. They deserve this dedicated time with you.

☐ Prepare any pertinent information that will make the time more useful and efficient.

☐ Be ready to share a few examples of the staffer having done an excellent job on work tasks.

☐ Think about ways you can support the staffer in their continued job or project success. Share during the session's closing minutes.

Possible questions (options):

What do you see as the best use of our time today?

Your situation sounds complex. How are you thinking about addressing it?

What options have you considered related to the concern you raised?

What are you seeing in this situation? Can you think of anything you may not be seeing or considering?

Look at this flow and sample dialogue. Adapt or use for ideas. This is set up for a 50–60-minute session.

This format allows you and your staff to look back and forward, share relevant updates, problem-solve, learn, and plan for the future. If you have less or more time, expand the time, eliminate or shorten a few items. Adapt as you go.

Minutes	The Flow (flexible)	Purpose
3	*Initiate and purpose*	Take a few moments to connect with the direct report's current state-- establishing rapport, before digging into key topics.
5	*Explore key topics (next 4 items)* To learn of and affirm what's working well in their work	*What's been going well since our last conversation?*
3	Confirm direct report's agenda and priority topics (to address during this session)	*What's the most important things we should talk about today?* These moments are the confirm the agenda.
10	To check accountability for anything the direct report committed to do during your last meeting (Be sure you or they have the list.)	*Can you give an update on the actions you agreed to take the last time we talked?*

15	Direct report's items This allows direct reports to have your ear and support as they address pressing work or career issues.	*How about looking at the topics you have?*
10-15	Leader's work updates to share (such as input, career growth, unique topics, etc.)	This should cover perceptions of performance; growth needs, any specific input needed. Include quick updates.
3	***Promises/ Next Steps*** These are the direct reports action steps in response to goals and challenges they are pursuing in their work	*What will you do specifically to move forward?*
5	Closing: Support. This shows the partnership role you play with your direct report. You can also suggest a way to support and ask whether that would be useful.	*Is there any support you'd like from me as you move forward?* *Thanks for this time. It makes a difference.* End on a good note and confirm next meeting.

Adjusting for unique topics: Some topics are best addressed individually with time set aside to do so.

- As noted earlier, that might include getting the direct report's thoughts and feedback on: work culture and climate, career development (see conversation guide #6), job satisfaction team needs, project planning, recognition of contributions, or debriefing the rationale for saying "No" to a request or more.

- You can address these by adjusting the agenda, especially the designated time for the leader.

Including these topics periodically in your one-on-ones can help you become aware of the state of their morale and how satisfied they are with their job. It can provide quality feedback; gather input on issues that impact them or the team; and uncover communication concerns. These topics help with staff retention and satisfaction.

Some questions that might be useful for special topics:

If you were to describe the climate or what it feels like to be on this team, what would you say?

How would you rate your overall morale on a scale of 1-10? What accounts for this rating?

What would make this the best place for you to work and give yourself more fully to our goals?

How would you describe your intent to stay with the organization over the short, moderate, and long-term? What factors influence your intent?

What thoughts do you have about topics that support the team's development over the next several months? What would add the most value?

Let's talk about the request you made that for now I won't be able to approve. I'd like us to explore that a bit and determine alternatives or next steps. What are your initial thoughts?

About recognition: Here I am offering a few words about recognition of progress and contributions because of the scant attention given to it. Supervisory leaders disproportionately pay more attention to the challenges than to what is working well, except to give the standard "great job" accolade.

Scheduling time periodically to go beyond the "great job" statements and provide specific, affirming feedback helps staff to 1) know, repeat, and enhance what they are already doing well, and 2) feel their contributions are notices and valued.

These are not "fluff" conversations, they are strategic in that they can inspire, develop, and improve work outcomes. People need to know what matters most and when and how they are excelling.

Suggestions:

- Spend time reviewing the employee's work products, processes, and relationships to create a list, allowing you to be specific in your appreciative feedback.

- When offering this recognition feedback, share with the staffer the value the specific contributions have for the team and the organization. (see sample chart below.)

Contribution: Specific product, process, or relationship	Value to the organization and/or team

As you share, these questions might be helpful:

What else would it take for you to continue being fully energized and productive in your work?

What do you believe are the sources of your positive approach and contributions to the organization? (This might help with engagement strategies for others.)

When you think about your success, what is one tip you would share with someone else to help them succeed?

In what ways can you engage your skills and talents better to bring you more satisfaction?

Closing thought: One-on-one meetings are a special time for the individual staffer. It's time just for them, and leaders should treat them with great regard.

You can turn these into meaningful, forward moving, clarifying, celebratory, and inspiring conversations. Do not allow your one-on-ones to become rote, perfunctory calendar appointments.

5. BUILD OR REPAIR A RELATIONSHIP

Healthy, constructive workplace relationships are essential for sustained high performance and the happiness and well-being of your staff and other stakeholders. Relationship building requires ongoing attention since we cannot assume a relationship's quality will be static and permanent. People change and may have new expectations, conflicts arise, ruptures are created, and harmful communication blunders happen. Then, there are new relationships you need to form as new staff or colleagues join your sphere of work or as roles change that can alter workplace power dynamics.

The need to repair bonds at work is inevitable. People won't always agree, and emotions and judgements are certain to surface. We, hopefully, recognize we aren't always right, and others don't always respond how we think they should. Skilled leaders are keenly aware that the health of the work culture depends on them repairing any breached relationships.

Situations for relationship building: to learn about people's motivations, priorities, background, and strengths; for partnerships where respectful relationships are critical to success; to repair a broken or strained relationship; getting to know a new team member or colleague to determine how to work together; to turn rivals into allies, and more.

Tips:

- ✓ When initiating these conversations, be sure to grant most of the time to your conversation partner. (Since you are trying to learn about them, center their experience).

- ✓ These conversations are often conducted in relaxed settings, i.e., morning coffees, lunches, i.e., when people tend to be less guarded.

- ✓ Determine what you want to "learn" from the conversation in advance and have questions in mind to move towards that learning.

- ✓ Review the tips on assessing your listening quotient (see pages 59-61) as you prepare.

Your preparation:

- ☐ Prepare a few questions to guide the dialogue to help accomplish what you want.

- ☐ It might be helpful to ask the conversation partner to bring 2-3 questions they believe would help build connections between you.

- ☐ Be ready to be a bit vulnerable, sharing parts of yourself (though not deeply personal aspects).

- ☐ In a relationship repair conversation, be ready to receive feedback constructively, with low defensiveness and openness to learn. (Review pages 55-58 on managing emotional triggers.)

Sample questions for relationship building in various situations. Adapt the ones to your situation.

What do you find most satisfying about your new job?

What differences have you noticed here when compared with your last job that you wish we had here?

How should we work together in a way that brings you the most satisfaction?

What are some of your preferences that would help you do your best work?

How would you describe the best aspects of our workplace so far?

What are the ways our work intersects? And what should we work on together more than we do now?

What would motivate you to stay here five years or more?

What does an ideal workday look like for you?

What would you like to see happen differently here?

What would you like to know about me that would make our working relationship more satisfying?

How should we fix things when they go wrong?

What have you learned recently that will be helpful in the future?

What was your thought process when you decided to move forward on the project the way you did?

What advice would you give if you were asked about how to make this the best place to work?

What are some of your skills and strengths you'd like to use more at work?

If you could trade one part of your work to do more of another part, what might that look like?

What do you most look forward to outside of work?

Questions that might help during a relationship repair conversation:

In what ways do you see us already on the same page about the issue?

What is the most important thing you need from me?

What would you like me to do differently when similar situations arise in the future?

How can we support each other in moving forward positively and with full engagement?

Remember feedback receptively is about *having the courage to see ourselves as others see us and to identify areas where we can improve.*

Look at this flow and sample dialogue. Adapt it or use it for ideas to meet your needs. Relationship building conversations are typically less formal and fluid than others. So, avoid taking a rigid approach.

1.	Initiate the conversation and state the topic	*Hello (name). I'm glad we have set aside this time to continue fostering good working relationships. That's important to me and to our work.* (This might change depending on the type of relationship building. If it's repair, be direct about that: *Hello xxx, I'm happy we made time to talk together to address the situation that seemed to create a rupture in our working relationship. I am very much hoping to move forward positively and figure out how to avoid the missteps from the past.*
2.	Explore how to proceed	*I have a few questions that might help us strengthen our connections.* *First, let me ask: Do you have any thoughts or expectations for this time we are spending?*
3.	Explore relationship building, guided by questions	Use the questions you prepared and their expectations to build connections. Depending on the time and receptivity, discern when you've covered enough. Show you are open and listening. They might want you to answer the same questions you are asking them; be willing to do so.

4. Summarize, Final Feedback and Agreements	*This has been meaningful time. I'm glad we did this. So, let's see what we've said that is most important to move forward productively as colleagues.* Summarize the ways you both suggested for strengthening the relationship. *Did I get that right?* After the review, you can start with your commitments, *I will....* *Before we close, is there anything else important that's not been said?* (Allow time to respond)
5. Wrap Up and Next Steps	*Again, thanks for the time. Feel free to reconnect when needed and I'll do the same.*

Closing thought: Relationship building conversations are profoundly human and dynamic. So, stay true to your goal of strengthening the relationship. That requires flexibility, genuineness, honesty, empathy, openness to novel approaches, and full presence. It generally takes a bit of time to build or strengthen bonds, so accept progress rather than an immediate ideal state for the relationship.

If it's a relationship REPAIR conversation, you might benefit from using the planning worksheet to think through it. (A blank one is on Page 156.)

6. CAREER DEVELOPMENT/ADVANCEMENT

Setting up periodic conversations with your staff members about career development is an important part of leading people. It is well-established that human potential is boundless; regrettably, however, much of it is untapped or underutilized at work. So, planning and anticipating requests for development and career growth is a proactive practice.

Career conversations offer a number of benefits. These include: indicating you believe in a learning culture that encourages ongoing growth; cultivating more positive relationships with you, the team, and the organization; helping staff take responsibility for thinking about and defining what career success looks like; fostering staff retention; and supporting the organization's preparation for future talent capital needs.

Situations: Staff career planning, requests for raises or promotions, prepare staffer for a promotion, identify growth needs to take their next career steps.

Tips:

✓ Schedule a career aspirations conversation at least once each year. The length is up to the staffer and you. (A 15-minute check-in may work for one staffer while a one-hour session works best for another).

✓ If possible, make career talks and annual performance review conversations separate to give each adequate attention.

✓ Do not avoid these talks due to concern that you may not be able to satisfy requests for advancement. Encourage staff to chart their own career trajectory. Then your role is to listen, learn, and support.

✓ Know that some people will be content with their current role, yet checking in shows you are concerned about their needs; plus, they may have aspects of their role that they would like altered to make it more satisfying.

✓ Career growth can be related to upward movement, lateral movement, current job enlargement, increased involvement in work-related networks, task groups, or committees, or new learning to bring freshness to the role.

✓ Think ahead and be vigilant.

> **People tend to seek a career change when they:** have long tenure in their job, missed out on a job they applied for, have a new supervisor, have a tough time with the work culture, experience work boredom, or complain of stress or feeling overworked.

✓ Since there are several types of career conversations, some might elicit different emotions, so plan accordingly.

Your preparation:

☐ Gather pertinent information and reflect on the staffer's background e.g., previous notes about career goals, areas of thriving, growth areas, resume, and current role tenure.

☐ Be up to date on the organization's emerging talent needs and new areas of work.

☐ Check the latest information about the types of new or emerging job roles and level of funding support the organization provides.

☐ Ask the direct report to prepare a few notes on their career goals, their strengths and any development needs that support the goals.

☐ Prepare to be open, curious, interested, and even anticipate being asked questions you might not be able to answer.

Optional questions for career conversations:

When you think about the next role you want to pursue, what areas of personal and professional growth do you believe would help you get there?

What are the challenges and opportunities that should be considered as you pursue this role?

What draws you to this opportunity?

What are some areas you'd like to pursue for learning and development to bring even more interest and challenge to your current work?

Look at this flow and sample dialogue. Adapt it or use it for ideas to structure your conversation.

1.	Initiate the conversation and state the topic	*Thanks for reaching out to have a conversation about your career goals.* Or, *I scheduled this time for us to talk about how you'd like your career to grow over the next year or so.*
2.	Explore (Leave time for them to respond between each of the questions)	*You've prepared some thoughts. Can you share them now?* *How do you see these recommendations for career growth directly supporting the organization's goals?* *In what ways are you already prepared to take these next steps?* *What else do you need to be ready for the next step?*
3.	Agreements	*Considering all that you've shared and the organization's guidelines, let's think about how we might move forward.* This can include your and their ideas.

4.	Set specific actions	*Let's set some concrete next steps.* Determine those and due dates.
5.	Wrap Up and Next Steps	*This has been helpful. Is there anything else we need to address before we close?* *When is a good time to check in on the next steps we established? Determine that:*_____. Close on a positive note.

Two special career topics:

  1. Request for promotion or salary increase:

While this may feel like a potentially anxiety-inducing conversation, relax and view it as an opportunity to demonstrate that you value the staffer or to provide them with feedback and support to grow into the salary or role they seek.

Be sure you are up to date on a) the company's salary scales and where your staff person is currently situated, b) the compensation policies, and 3) your budget to determine what might or might not be possible at this time or a later time.

For the direct report making the request, ask them to prepare some notes on: 1) the rationale for their request, identifying what they see as their value-adding, above and beyond performance to date, and

2) what they envision as their added organizational contributions or bodies of work that would validate this elevation.

Enter the conversation with openness and receptivity. You can think about what you hear during the conversation to help decide how to move forward. For example: *"Hello xxx, I am happy to spend some time with you to talk through your request for elevating your role in the organization."* (Then proceed with the Tips, Preparation, and adjust, as needed, the Sample Flow presented here (Conversation 6).

2. *Almost ready for the promotion*

There are times when a staffer demonstrates most of the skills and behaviors for advancement, but a few minor concerns are getting in the way of the promotion. You have avoided addressing them for fear they might feel diminished. In a situation I've come across, the leader's thought was *I support promoting one of my leaders but there are some things she needs to do first. I haven't talked to her about them.*

Like that leader, your internal dialogue might then be:

- *Does she know these skill or interpersonal gaps exist and why they matter?*

- *Does she know I see her value to the team and that I have my intention set on promoting her?*

- *What does the right conversation look like and how will I initiate it?*

That particular conversation can follow the general format. Determine how you will *Initiate* and *Explore* the promotion request with her, using questions presented in Conversation 6 or creating your own. Remember in the initiate portion, it's best to be clear and use positive framing, such as:

Hello Joyce. I'm glad we set aside time to talk about the possibility of promoting you to the role you want. You are on track for that. With a few changes, I think we will get there. You are already demonstrating the new role's requirement of xxxx (specify). That's great. I am concerned about a few specific matters where you need a bit of work. Let's talk about that and how to get there.

Proceed with these conversation topics using the same format already offered.

Closing thoughts: To support staff retention, staff thriving, and future talent needs, give forethought and arrange career planning conversations on a periodic basis. Don't wait until your staffers check out, i.e., quietly quit. When staff feel they have opportunities to gain experience, their talents are respected and valued, and they have pathways for their compensation and influence to grow, they are likely to feel high satisfaction with themselves, your leadership, and the organization.

7. BEHAVIOR/POOR INTERACTION PATTERNS

Another common one-on-one conversation that is often troubling, avoided or managed poorly is related to a direct report's pattern of poor or ineffective interactions. Their tendency may be an indicator of their underdeveloped interpersonal competence or something else that's affecting them. These, often thoughtless, behavioral incidences come with a cost that increases over time when unaddressed.

Getting to the root of this behavior can help activate the staffer to make adaptations to more emotionally mature self-expression. Building your direct report's awareness that exhibiting situationally unsuitable behavior or conduct that transgresses professional parameters can have a potentially wide-reaching impact—on the workplace and their longer-term success. Offering them a chance to expand their behavioral repertoire by practicing other ways to respond is a worthy outcome for such a conversation.

Much is at stake. Avoiding chronic patterns can lead to several undesirable consequences: relationships can be damaged, people avoid interacting with them, and the team culture can become toxic. So set your mind to the belief that addressing these behaviors can be a supportive mechanism for your team members to thrive.

Studies have shown respondents believe[30] providing *"corrective feedback improves their performance when it is presented well."*

Situations/scenarios: a habit of public rude language, chronic lateness to key meetings, talking over people or dominating during meetings, poorly executed presentations, disclosing confidential information, overt hostility with colleagues, disruptive behavior long tolerated, public defensiveness, negativity.

Tips:

- ✓ If it's an out-of-character behavior, address it simply by taking the staffer aside and asking about the behavior and how to manage better the next time. This is different than a pattern.

- ✓ Always address these patterns privately to avoid public embarrassment unless someone is publicly being mistreated; here, step in to be clear it is unacceptable treatment.

- ✓ Be open to listening to the person's perspective, which may help you understand and address the issues at hand.

- ✓ Do not label words of dissent as dysfunctional unless the communication is disrespectful. However, chronic contrariness might benefit from a private conversation to get to the root of

---

[30] Zenger Folkman, 2019, Feedback: The Powerful Paradox, accessed at zengerfolkman.com

the staffer's disenchantment and its impact along with better ways to assert their views.

✓ Do not spend time re-hashing an extensive list of examples, which can debilitate the staffer; the aim is to be clear on the issue, and the greater purpose is how to move forward.

✓ Get right to the issue. Don't drag, linger, or sugar-coat it. The first few minutes are critical to moving from clarifying the issue, its impact, then towards the best resolution.

Your Preparation:

☐ For this conversation, utilize the Planning Worksheet (p. 134) to help you think through it.

☐ Steady yourself so you deliver the feedback calmly, humanely, and directly. If the staffer responds defensively, be ready to assure them that this conversation is intended to be a support for their success at work. Don't join in a defensive battle; pause, breathe, continue.

☐ Try to let go of any thought that this person deliberately set out to bring harm.

☐ Plan your opening well. According to <u>Fierce Conversations</u>,[31] you should try to do the following within the first 60-75 seconds:

• Name the issue.

---

[31] Scott, S. Fierce Conversations, pg. 148-162

- Provide a specific example that illustrates the behavior that needs to change.
- Describe the feelings it causes (optional).
- Clarify what's at stake.
- Identify how you have contributed to the behavioral issue not being solved.
- Indicate your wish to resolve it.
- Invite the staffer to respond.

Here's an example of an opening, based on applying <u>Fierce Conversation</u>'s recommendation:

Marie, I want to talk about the effect your style of interacting with the team has on our team's working relationships. I have observed you cutting people off and insisting on your way during a number of situations. I have also heard reports that people feel like they should not express their views because of this habit. I'm disappointed that this kind of interaction makes our meetings less productive than they could be. I want to be clear that a lot is at stake: we are not hearing great ideas that might be helpful, people sense there are no behavioral boundaries, and our forward movement is hindered because our meetings are not very productive. I admit I was reluctant to address this with you sooner; that's my mistake. I should have clarified professional expectations and norms. I want to resolve this so we can move forward. Can you share your views about what is happening and what we can do to resolve this?

After that, the conversation is ready to move forward using the conversation flow addressed in chapter 4, i.e., explore, agreements, next steps and close.

Some questions (options):

What's your sense of how this type of behavior affects our working environment?

What are your initial reactions to the issues raised?

If you were to be completely open, what about this is something you've heard before?

What do you think is causing you to behave in this way?

If someone from the outside observed this situation, how might it reflect on you and the team?

How can we move forward to ensure more constructive interactions?

What might be some alternative responses when you feel yourself beginning to display this behavior?

Look at this sample dialogue addressing poor interaction patterns. Adapt it or use it for ideas to structure your conversation.

1.	Initiate the conversation and state the topic	*I'd like to talk with you about a behavior you may not be aware of that detracts from the work and your stature as a valued staff.*

2.	Explore	*The behaviors I am thinking about are:* (state clearly only a few and most critical).
		Can you share a bit about your awareness of such behaviors and how they might impact the work environment and teamwork?
		Provide time to have them share. Remain calm.
		Share the impact you see the behaviors having on the team
		I want to re-set how we move forward to address these behaviors so you can let your strengths shine through better. Also, we want to have a positive environment as we do our work, so reinforcing professional behavioral norms is key to that.
		What steps can you take to address them? Allow time for them to share their suggested next steps.
3.	Summarize and Agreements	*How can I be helpful in supporting you?*
		Are there any resources you need?

		So, for clarity, how will you move forward differently in the future?
		If you have a few ideas, you can share those as well.
		Summarize, for clarity, the specific changes the staffer agreed to make.
		Clarify why it matters and expectations for professional behavior and boundaries.
4.	Wrap Up and Next Steps	*This time has been helpful. Is there anything else we need to address before closing?* *Let's check back on progress after our next team meeting on_____.*
		Close on a respectful note.

Closing Thoughts: It's not that unusual to see these types of unhealthy work interactions on display. What's at issue is how you address them productively and maintain healthy work relationships. Engaging in conversations about low quality and emotionally damaging interactions counts most when you and that employee NEED to work together. These conversations offer a chance to re-set boundaries that foster respect, trust, and better collaboration.

Use the worksheet to think through this kind of often difficult conversation.

Plan and Practice Worksheet

What's the conversation topic? _____

Who is your conversation with? _____

Why does it matter to have this conversation and now?

_____

_____

1) How much time will you set for the conversation?
   15 minutes○ 30 minutes ○ an hour ○ other: ○

2) Where will you have it? _____

3) What information will be used for this conversation?

4) What are the best outcomes for both you and your
   conversation partner? What should be clear

5) What could possibly make the conversation go off
   track, and how might you respond if that happens?

6) What are some reminders to yourself to help you
   manage yourself well?
   a.
   b.

7) What's an effective way to open (*initiate*) the conversation?

8) What is a possible flow (agenda) for the conversation (to *clarify purpose and explore the issue*)?

a.

b.

c.

d.

e.

f.

9) Agreements (*promises*): Be sure to end with agreements and clear, specific next steps. (Identify during the meeting and make note of them here)

Action	By whom?	By when?

10) What will be your approach to closing/wrapping up the conversation (i.e., ending well)? _____
_____

8. PERFORMANCE CHECKPOINTS

These periodic checkpoint engagements are valuable in that they help remove the typical foreboding staffers bear when the annual appraisal occurs. Staff should not have to guess all year long about how well you believe they are performing. Thus, having a series of conversations on progress, challenges, support needed, and any adjustments makes a meaningful difference.

Checkpoints could be part of your one-on-one meetings—at bi-monthly or quarterly intervals. Such periodic checkpoints provide staff with enough time and support to correct any performance shortfalls as well as to celebrate what's working.

These two-way conversational checkpoints can be somewhat informal, then more formal when related to the organization's official annual appraisal.

Situations: One of a series of individual sessions to examine the state of success on performance goals (bi-monthly, quarterly, semi-annually)

Tips:

- ✓ Determine the cadence of checkpoints and communicate those to your staff persons.

✓ Using the regularly scheduled one-on-one meeting or part of it as a checkpoint (15-20 minutes) should be sufficient when you and your direct report have done the preparation suggested below.

✓ Don't forget to honor positive results to date.

✓ As needed, be flexible adjusting some of the goals in cases where you realize they might have been unreasonable, or the staffer is facing extenuating circumstances.

✓ Verify if there are company requirements for performance reviews, periodic and annual. Comply with those.

✓ Be direct if you have concerns about the employee's progress to date and focus on getting them to identify strategies to address deficiencies as they go forward.

✓ Spend most of the time being future focused since these checkpoints leave the staffer some time to strengthen their work outputs.

Preparation:

☐ **Before the conversation, ask your direct report to do a bit of preparation:** *Next week, when we talk, let's check in on your progress towards your annual goals. I'm doing this with everyone to ensure people have what they need to succeed. Can you take a look at your goals and* *have a few comments about where you are on each of them and bring ideas on how you plan to achieve the goals going forward?*

☐ Review the direct report's current status on goal attainment.

For this conversation, simply follow the flow of the general conversation guide and during the Explore part, interject questions such as these that follow.

Possible questions (options):

What would it take for you to meet and exceed the expectations we set at the beginning of the year?

What does performance excellence look like to you?

What words would you use to describe how you feel about your progress to date?

If you could have one barrier removed that would allow you to achieve even more, what would that be?

Look at this flow and sample dialogue. Adapt it to meet your needs.

1. Initiate the conversation and state the topic	Use regular one-on-one meeting opening or *"This is a checkpoint to reflect on where you are on your annual performance goals. It's a chance to acknowledge progress, determine how to move forward successfully and exchange ideas that help ensure*

		you are successful in achieving your performance outcomes.
2.	Explore	Use the prepared goals and objectives and ask the staffer: *Why not walk through what you prepared in regard to the annual goals and where you are to date?* *How do you feel about where you are?* *How would you describe your level of certainty about achieving or exceeding the goals by year-end?* (Listen to their input) *Thanks for your thoughts. They are helpful.* *I'd like to share a few thoughts on what I'm seeing as well* (only if there is a difference in what they expressed. If you have concerns, express them). Otherwise, confirm and make a few comments on the importance of achieving the goals for the department and organization.
3.	Agree on current state of goal progress	*What should be some next steps to ensure you are on track to achieve the goals?*

		Agree on these and confirm any timelines related to them. *Is there anything you need from me at this time?*
4.	Wrap Up and Next Steps	*This has been helpful. Let's check in again on how well your strategies are going as you work to achieve the goals. What about us revisiting this in a month?_____ (or do you suggest a different time?)* Close session on a positive note.

Closing thoughts: With year-round practices in place, the annual performance appraisal results become predictable (not shocking nor contentious). Investing in these periodic goal checkpoints relieves stress for you and your direct reports and builds better bonds between the two of you. These can be celebratory when expectations are being met or exceeded. On the other hand, these can be preventive, allowing people time to improve their performance before year end.

9. RECOGNITION AND CONTRIBUTIONS

It is understood that skilled supervisory leaders have regularly scheduled conversations with their direct reports to check in, support their projects, confer about performance, exchange ideas, build connections, correct missteps, and more. It is rare, however, that a specific time is reserved where the primary focus is on recognizing progress and staffers' exceptional contributions.

Do you want to deepen engage and inspire continued good work results? Then, send your staffer a calendar invitation to sit with you for 30 minutes to talk about their work excellence or progress on a specific target. For some leaders, this will require deliberate intent since leaders tend to offer more corrective (i.e., negative) than positive feedback. And even those leaders known to recognize accomplishments on the spot (and you should), having these <u>scheduled</u> conversations will be a new practice.

Situations: Progress on a project, outstanding performance of specific tasks, highlight strengths, annual recognition (year in review), positive changes in attitude or interactions.

There are myriad rationales, fears, or barriers associated with offering increasing amounts of direct, positive feedback and recognition. Among them: *They might expect a raise soon if I give too much positive feedback; this is what they come to work and get paid to do; they are good but could still do better; this might give them an exaggerated sense of themselves; there are too many other pressing needs to spend time on this; they might stop working as hard, etc.*

Recognition of progress and valued contribution is a motivator for high engagement and performance.

> *"If an employee achieves more and her manager reinforces her performance, the employee is likely to strive harder and reach increasingly higher levels of performance."* [32]

Tips:

✓ Have specific facts, situations, and reasoning related to why the contributions matter.

✓ Be able to name the strengths and skills you see the person applying in their work.

✓ Determine who *might not* benefit from this type of conversation, so as not to give mixed signals, e.g., a chronic low-performing employee who may be transitioned out of the organization soon.

✓ Besides these scheduled conversations, offering positive feedback should be an ongoing practice and provided close to the time of the situation warranting recognition.

---

[32] Zenger, J. and Folkman, J. 2009. The Extraordinary Coach, p. 185

✓ Do not reduce their contributions to simplistic or trivial issues.

✓ Since you will ask the employee's thoughts about their contributions during your annual and quarterly review checkpoints, do not ask them to bring anything. This is their time to hear from you.

Preparation:

☐ Set a frequency for an overall recognition and contributions private conversation. Will you do this semi-annually or annually?

☐ Review the period being covered and pay attention to the substantive contributions. Prepare a list of those and projects done well. (Consider tangible results and interpersonal strengths and core values applied to carry out the work.)

Possible questions (options):

What reactions do you have to what I have shared with you about your contributions and their value?

To what extent does receiving positive feedback matter to you?

Which of your interpersonal strengths do you feel you're successfully applying to help get your and the team's work done?

Do you see this differently? Are there other contributions that I might have missed that bring you great pride?

Suggested flow: Adapt as appropriate.

1.	Initiate the conversation and state the topic	*Thanks for joining me for about 30 minutes to talk specifically about what's going exceptionally well with your work, team contributions, and your strengths that are showing up at work.*
2.	Explore	*I'd like to go through what I've experienced. I want you to know I, the team and the organization value a number of your contributions. I have a list.* The list should walk through either a specific project and its value or other specific contributions. Go through what you have and why it matters.
		How do you feel about what I've shared? Allow them time to share their thoughts. *Are there other accomplishments you'd like to bring to my attention?*

		Allow them time to share their thoughts.
3.	Agreements	*Thanks for your thoughts. Do you have any questions for me about what I've shared?*
		Do we need any follow up?
4.	Wrap Up and Next Steps	*I appreciate your time. This has been a pleasure. And I look forward to your continued contributions even as we may face new challenges and opportunities. Your work matters.*
		Close session on a positive note.

Closing thoughts: Recognition of contributions and exceptional accomplishments motivates staffers for long-term high performance. It also signals to your team members the kinds of work, behaviors, and show of core values you and the organization need and respect. Overall, this is a chance to break the pattern of focusing on mostly negative behaviors and instead reinforce what is working and build on that.

10. TEAM CONVERSATIONS/MEETINGS

The most admired leaders plan and execute their staff meetings with the intent of them delivering value commensurate with the resource investment these gatherings consume. Effective leaders focus on individual and team development simultaneously. They are mindful that their one-on-one staff activities can be thwarted when team engagements are divisive, waste time, and fail to foster collective learning and shared norms.

Shifting team sessions from routinized gatherings to productive, growth oriented, and team strengthening sessions will pay off.

> *"Team-level development creates a shared language, shared commitments, and most importantly, a support system that reinforces new behaviors. When an entire team grows together, the impact is deeper and more sustainable."*[33]

Situations: Regularly scheduled team meetings, input and decision-making sessions, team retreats, team development and culture building, strategy sessions, project planning, and updates.

---

[33] Why team development outperforms individual growth, June 12, 2025, accessed at zengerfolkman.com

Many team projects or engagements under-deliver, resulting in less than the sum of all of the talent in the room often due to interpersonal friction and poor conversation processes. To get started, consider this simple statement:

> *"A good meeting is usually determined before it starts."*[34]

Tips:

✓ Have a clear purpose for each meeting. Think: *WHY are we meeting? What work do we want this meeting to accomplish? What do I need the team to think through?* If those can't be answered, ask yourself: *Do we need a meeting*?

✓ Identify the purpose of the meeting, e.g., to review or improve a process, generate ideas on a novel challenge, make a decision, build team synergies, emergency meeting on an issue that impacts everyone, retreat for strategic thinking and team building, launch and motivate for a new goal, etc.

✓ Have at least one compelling agenda item during the meeting that builds interest, draws on the thinking of the team, and is relevant to the work. Here are some examples:

• *We want to dedicate some time to getting your thoughts on how we can better retain our clients.*

---

[34] VandeHei, J, Allen, M, et al., 2022. Smart Brevity, p. 136

- *Let's take 20 minutes to explore what equity should look like in our organization.*

- *Let's brainstorm ideas on how to support the new strategic initiatives.*

- *What does elevating our work look like for us?*

- *What should our learning agenda include this year to enhance our work and support the new objectives?*

- *If we have to do more with less, how can we think and act differently to do that productively and without overburdening ourselves?*

- *When you think of well-being, a value of the organization, what does that look like?*

- *How do we bring our core values to life in our team and our work?*

- *If we had to choose what aspects of our work to do more of and less of to be more efficient, what would those be?*

✓ To prepare team members for the gathering prompt some pre-thinking by distributing a short pre-read (e.g., article or chapter) so they are informed and ready to be involved.

✓ Share roles with team members related to planning and *leading* the meetings. This builds team efficacy. It works best when the leader provides everyone with specific parameters, so the meeting purpose maintains its focus.

✓ Limit the number of agenda items so you are able to focus on what you set out to achieve.

✓ Keep status update meetings to a minimum since it's simply information. If you do have updates, keep them short and follow up with email to ensure everyone has the updates.

✓ Provide and try to stick to timeframes for the agenda topics so all items are covered. If some items need to go over the time allotted, agree to reschedule some topics for future meetings.

✓ Consider which aspects of the meeting will 1) strengthen bonds and 2) engage team talents.

✓ Continuity: Connect previous meetings to the next so the team can see they are moving towards some specific objectives. At the start of each meeting, review what was addressed in the last meeting and report on previously assigned actions.

✓ Summarize decisions, next steps, and who is responsible at the close of meetings.

Preparation:

☐ Prepare and send the agenda out, if possible, a week (or more) before the team session. Check with those you want to co-lead a portion to be sure they agree to do so and are clear. Identify and attach any pre-think questions or reading that address a key meeting topic.

☐ Assign someone to record action steps that emerge during the meeting. Before you close, decide who will do the actions and by when.

Sample questions for meaningful meetings (options):

What would we need to accomplish by the end of this meeting to say it was meaningful and productive?

What is the next level of thinking we need to do on this issue before us?

If there's one thing that hasn't been said to reach the best understanding of the issue, what is it?

What would it take to create the change we seek?

Is this an issue that requires a resolution or can we live without one for now? What's at stake if anything?

What challenges might come our way, and how might we meet them?

What should our process for resolving conflicts among team members be?

Look at this flow and sample dialogue. Adapt it or use it for ideas for your conversation.

1.	Initiate, state the purpose, build connections	*Welcome everyone to our (weekly, monthly, or annual) team gathering. It's always a pleasure to have everyone here to contribute to our important work and think together to improve it.* *xxx (team member name) will take a few minutes to build our connections.* Connection activity (if one hour meeting, use no more than 10 minutes, if all day, this can take 30-45 minutes to do something more substantive.) *Everyone has our agenda for our gathering. Let's review it so we all know where we are headed.* (Quickly review it and who's leading sections). *Are we missing anything critical?* (Allow input and modify agenda if needed.)
2.	Explore the main topics	Go through the agenda items, paying attention to time. Each agenda item should have a purpose and closing. Record any action steps that come out of the topics.
3.	Agreements	*I hope everyone feels this meeting was productive. Let's do a thumbs up, thumbs down to take the temperature.*

	My goal is for every one of our meetings to be a good use of our time and resources. Summarize the meeting purpose and what was covered to achieve that purpose. (1-2 minutes) *What was most useful for you today?* *Next, let's go through next steps and confirm who will do what?* Remember:

Action step	Who	By when

4. Wrap Up and Next Steps	Announce the next meeting date. Closing thoughts: This can be assigned to a team member in advance (1-2 minutes) Or simply thank everyone for their time and valuable input. Close session on a positive note.

One special team conversation topic: Occasionally, you will need to **mediate a conflict** between staff members. Initially, you would ask the staffers to try to resolve the issue themselves. If they prefer or need you to be involved, clarify your role is not to solve it independently but to help them to 1) build their problem-solving skills, 2) apply their EQ skills to constructively mediate the conflict, and 3) return to at least a "good enough" stasis to be able to work together respectfully.

Possible questions for mediating conflict between staffers (Do not absolve them of responsibility to remedy <u>their</u> issue; provide support, remind them what's at stake, and help them constructively address the issues.)

What might be at the root of the issue?

What does a good resolution look like to each of you?

What would someone with a vastly different view than either of you say about this?

How would you describe your role in this situation?

What accountability will you accept for restoring productive, respectful relations with your colleague?

What are the best next steps for resolving this issue as we move forward?

Closing thoughts: Team meetings should, for the most part, be conversations rather than update sessions. They are times for you to talk WITH the team about substantive topics. These meetings can be powerful sources to learn, develop new skills, innovate new processes, make decisions, and bolster team spirit and constructive collaboration behaviors.

In Closing

You've come to the end of *Better Conversations for Better Results, A Leader's Guide to Skillful Work Conversations.* What I believe, for sure, is that as leaders, we must have enough confidence in our capabilities and identity to balance these with enough humility to keep learning and evolving our interpersonal competence.

As leaders, we are each tasked with helping others grow and possibly rise to places beyond which we will ascend. We can facilitate the development of those in our spheres of influence, especially those we lead directly, through compelling, consequential, transformational, and humane conversations individually and in groups.

To have such powerful conversations, begin embodying exceptional conversationalist skills. What might seem exceptional now—once you've elevated your capacity for leading and engaging in better conversations—will soon become the norm for your work interactions. Strive for conversations that connect, inspire, create, transform, and achieve.

Hopefully, these pages have helped you get there.

Lindune A. Lester

Plan and Practice Worksheet

What's the conversation topic? _____

Who is your conversation with? _____

Why does it matter to have this conversation and now?

_____

_____

1) How much time will you set for the conversation?
   15 minutes○ 30 minutes ○ an hour ○ other: ○

2) Where will you have it? _____

3) What information will be used for this conversation?

4) What are the best outcomes for both you and your
   conversation partner? What should be clear

5) What could possibly make the conversation go off
   track, and how might you respond if that happens?

6) What are some reminders to yourself to help you
   manage yourself well?
   a.
   b.

7) What's an effective way to open (*initiate*) the conversation?

8) What is a possible flow (agenda) for the conversation (to *clarify purpose and explore the issue*)?

a.

b.

c.

d.

e.

f.

9) Agreements (*promises*): Be sure to end with agreements and clear, specific next steps. (Identify during the meeting and make note of them here)

Action	By whom?	By when?

10) What will be your approach to closing/wrapping up the conversation (i.e., ending well)? _____
_____

Acknowledgements

I am immensely grateful to those leaders who chose me as their coaching partner. You have allowed me access to some of your innermost thoughts, joys, anxieties, and aspirations. You have given me a view of the "real" work of leaders in today's complex environment. Thank you, and I hope these stories and strategies will continue to be useful to you.

There are several people who have supported this work through the years and for whom I am grateful. These include foremost my writing partner and husband, Sondai K. Lester; my daughter Noni, a people and talent officer whose stories provide a glimpse into mid-level leaders and managers world, challenges, and frustrations along their direct reports who either suffer or find inspiration from them. These stories have influenced this book too.

To my friends, who are there to bounce my ideas around with, thank you for your ear and attention when we could be talking about travel, food, entertainment, aging gracefully, and love. The main ones are Jackie Gordon, Patricia Rencher, Cynthia Ward, and Diane Jackson.

And finally, I appreciate the new relationships I have built with fellow executive coaches, to learn what they're seeing and doing to advance the work of leaders in today's world.

About the Author

Lindiwe Stovall Lester spent 40 years doing *the people work* described in *The Everyday Leader* and *The People Smart Leader*. She is partner with top and mid-level leaders-- coaching and mentoring as they increase their mastery leading and inspiring others for high achievement. As president of Tap In Consulting, she limits her work of transformation to executive and leadership coaching, and team realignment and development consulting.

She retired as a national nonprofit senior leader, partnering with chief executives and their boards of directors. Her body of work centered on executive development, executive transition, strategic thinking and planning, board effectiveness, and enhancing the competencies of those in consulting roles.

A lifelong learner, Lindiwe makes sure she includes people from multiple generations in her circle to both enliven her understanding and stay abreast of changes and trends. A committed advocate for access and inclusion, Ms. Lester remains involved in coaching and mentoring leaders-of-color.

Lindiwe holds master's and post-master's degrees in instructional and human performance systems. She is certified in executive coaching, performance consulting, social and emotional intelligence, behavior analytics, and executive presence coaching.

Her family and friends, writing, art, and travel assume big spaces in her re-fired retirement life.

Index

(Look at the detailed Table of Contents first. These Index items are extra topics, listed here to make them easier to locate.)